Life's Memorable Moments

MICHAEL McGARREY

TACTICAL 16
PUBLISHING

Published by Tactical 16 Publishing

Colorado Springs, Colorado

www.Tactical16.com

ISBN: 978-1-943226-69-6 (paperback)

This wouldn't be possible without Jamie Tidwell. When I began to consider writing a book, she gave me the resources to do so. Thank you, Jamie, your kindness will now be known for as long as words are printed.

To my oldest sister, Andree. Thank you for always carrying my flag.

Thank you to all the teachers, college professors, and anyone else who told me I had a gift that needed to be shared.

Lastly, thank you to Geep Mechanical and everyone who worked there with me both those living and those who have "...shuffled off this mortal coil." I wouldn't have become the man I am without some hard-learned lessons and, more importantly, I wouldn't have lived a life worth writing about.

INTRODUCTION

"Life's Memorable Moments" is a collection of short but true stories I have told countless times. I usually tell them around campfires, at random social gatherings, to a girl to break an awkward silence, or to loved ones of those no longer living. The stories can be read individually or in order. They are all meant to give the reader some much-needed laughter. There are a few serious moments that are generally used to set up something to follow. Some of the names have been changed or omitted either by the person's request, because I couldn't contact them, or, in the case of my family members, to save them from unwanted fame if the book does better than expected.

I was the fifth child born to an Irish father and Italian mother. My siblings are two sisters, both born on September 11 but one year apart in 1963 and 1964, and two brothers. My oldest brother was born in 1966 and the other in 1968. Then I came along in the summer of 1980. Needless to say, my upbringing was a bit different than other kids my age. The stories of my childhood are punctuated with interesting moments. One, a little more relevant to the stories that follow, was when I won my first pool game at nine years old.

From the age of four, my father took me to the Oui Lounge with him. My entertainment was the bartender unlocking the pool table in the back room and letting me have free access to the pool balls while my dad and uncle sat at the bar. Staying in the backroom of the Oui, I would pull a chair around the pool table to stand on and use my hands to knock the balls around. As I grew, I began using a pool cue. One night in 1989, my mom, dad, and some of their friends were up at the bar, and I began playing against some college kids in the back room. I asked one guy if he wanted to play me for a cherry Coke, a Coke with actual cherries in it, and he agreed. I don't know if he let me win, but after I beat him, he took me to my parents to tell them I had just won and that he owed me a Coke. My father was proud, but my mother was pissed, mostly at my father for bringing me to the Oui enough that I had become that good at pool, but also at me for gambling at the age of nine. Needless to say, that ended my days of playing pool against college kids for Cokes.

In high school, I worked in a cafeteria my mother managed called Colonial Cafeteria. I had grown up working at the different cafeteria locations as a busboy, beginning at the age of fourteen. By the time I entered the work program my junior year of high school, I had trained as a baker and other roles in the cafeteria, including cashier. This was before the era of cashier machines that calculated the change for you. My mother allowed me to work thirty-nine hours a week, the max for a student, and I was paid minimum wage, which was $4.15 an hour. The minimum wage was plenty, though, because my only expenses were liability insurance and gas, which was only eighty-eight cents a gallon. There was also my social life, which consisted of gambling while playing pool at the bowling alley and entrance fees to compete in bull riding events.

I rode bulls all through high school and into the first year I worked at Geep Mechanical. I eventually quit bull riding when an injury resulted in missing some work. My boss told me I would need to choose between plumbing and bull riding. After some thought, I decided to keep following the more secure paycheck and quit riding bulls. But even now that I am in my forties, when I see a rodeo on TV or go to the Fort Worth Stock Show and Rodeo, the teenager in my heart misses the thrill of the chutes.

I hate to say that I was a typical bull rider in my youth, but I was in most ways. I was cocky, hot-headed, and though I wasn't eager to fight, I wasn't afraid of one either. When I started at Geep, I carried those character flaws with me. Luckily, the construction world in the late 1990s and early 2000s was still full of men tougher than axe handles who were eager to teach a young punk some life lessons the hard way.

Though the men were hard on me, they were also incredibly patient. There were many times, early on, I should have been fired. Instead, Geep Mechanical chose to chalk my mistakes up to being young and stupid and turned my mistakes into important life lessons. One such lesson was about a month after I had been hired.

I had a habit of always being at least ten minutes late, and after several warnings, enough was enough. Rather than fire me one Monday when I finally arrived at a construction site in Dallas, thirty-minutes late, the plumbing foreman, Old Man Tom as I referred to him, came out to my truck and said, "This job starts at 7:00 a.m. Go home. You can try again tomorrow."

I pulled into the parking lot at 7:00 a.m. on the dot the next day. Again, Tom came to my truck and said, "This job starts at 7:00 a.m., not 7:01. Go home. You can try again tomorrow."

I got to the site at 6:50 a.m. and closed my eyes for a quick nap in my truck. Tom woke me at 7:01 a.m. and said, "The job starts at 7:00 a.m. That means you're working at 7:00, not sleeping in your truck. Go home. You can try again tomorrow."

The next day I arrived at 6:45 a.m. I had all the job trailers unlocked and was working by 6:55 a.m. I won't say I was never late again, but if I was late, I called ahead of time, and there was a damn good reason.

The group I worked with were hard, but they were fair. It was a time before people were overly sensitive and worried about being offended. You better not let it show if you were offended because people would pick at what offended you until it was no longer a bother.

This volume of "Life's Memorable Moments" takes place after I graduated from high school in 1999 and began working as a plumber's helper at Geep Mechanical. It continues until I went on vacation to New York City in 2004.

I hope that you get a lot of laughs as you read this. I hope at times you think, "Damn, they really messed with him," but still laugh. And when it's all done, I hope that you remember it's still okay to laugh, especially at yourself, because that's all a person can do most of the time

CHAPTER 1

SOMETHING ABOUT FISHING

I am not sure how old I was when I first started fishing; however, I remember precisely when I became addicted to the endless pursuit of a perfect strike and hook set.

It was early summer in 1991; I was ten and ¾, so basically, I was eleven. My father, a friend of his, Charlie Freeman, and I were out at a hunting property near Hico, Texas. Nothing was in season, but we were shooting a .22 caliber rifle and fishing in a little stock tank. They were drinking Budweiser, and I had some "real" Dr. Pepper. After we ran through the ammo and cleaned the rifle, I grabbed my rod and reel and tore off to the stock tank.

Okay, I'll stop here for a second to catch some of my readers up on the terminology above.

A "stock tank" is just a large water storage area, made out of dirt and rock, built by ranchers to hold water so their cattle can drink. They are often "stocked" with an assortment of fish to keep the ponds relatively aerated and living.

"Real" Dr. Pepper was, as my father had told me, Dr. Pepper made with real sugar, bottled but not canned, and purchased at the first Dr. Pepper bottling plant located in Dublin, Texas.

Now, let us continue.

By the time I started fishing, it was late morning, and the temperature dial was steadily climbing toward that one-hundred-degree mark. But never underestimate the determination of a nearly eleven-year-old boy with a fishing pole. I was using a large spinnerbait lure and making long casts out to the center of the tank, then reeling back in at different speeds. The hope was to piss off a largemouth bass enough to cause a strike. After an hour or so with zero success, other than clearing the pond of moss and weeds, Charlie called out, "Toss it under that tree to the left."

Without delay, I did as instructed and, sure as hell, I caught the tree! With a few expletives whispered under my breath, I stood there bewildered at my current predicament. It wasn't my first tree problem, but this time the lure was dangling precariously over the water on an extremely small limb of a mesquite tree. I had learned from a previous tree climbing experience that mesquite trees have thorns; so, I said to myself, "the heck with it" and gave the line a quick tug. Much to my surprise, it did a couple of flips, unwrapping from the limb, and dropped right into the water. Again, I stood there, bewildered at what I just witnessed. "I can't believe that worked," I thought.

There was no time for self-reflection, though, because the line on my reel was humming away, causing the drag to sing. I jerked back on the rod and set the hook. The fight was on. My rod tip bent significantly enough to cause Charlie and my dad to come over and watch the event.

Almost as if cued by a director, the creature made its unveiling to the audience. It broke through the surface of the water with a fury. It was at this moment I uttered my first words of profanity in front of an adult.

"Holy shit!" I yelled. My father responded instantly with, "What was that?" I responded equally as quickly with, "No time to talk important CHit going on here!" He and Charlie laughed, so I figured I was in the clear. Time to focus! It only counts as a catch if you land it, and this whale was far from caught.

The fight continued long enough for Charlie to replace the now empty beers. As he returned, I was wading out in the water to free the beast from the moss and weeds near the bank. I strode out of the tank, fish in my right hand, pole in my left, and my chest extending three feet before me. Charlie took my rod, and I removed the lure from the fish's mouth. I stood there in front of Charlie and my dad holding my trophy. No photos were taken, but a photo could not have captured the moment well enough anyway.

That night around the fire, I wasn't just a spectator to the stories; I now had my own. Charlie and Dad sat there, listened, laughed, and engaged me in conversation. I was now not just my father's son, but one of the guys.

It was at that moment, though, when my real addiction began. I would seek that feeling feverishly, and although I would go on to catch many more fish, none would compare to that moment, until my mid-thirties when that feeling came rushing back, and I was that almost eleven-year-old boy again.

Around the age of twelve, I saw a movie that would change my fishing quests forever, "A River Runs Through It." The movie introduced me to a new fishing style, fly fishing. The beauty of a fly-fishing cast is what captured my imagination. It showed me that there could be more to fishing than just throwing a lure in the water and reeling it in. There was an art to fly fishing, to perfecting the cast in order to present the fly in just the right manner, so it sits on top of the water coaxing a fish to rise for the strike. This gave casting as much enjoyment as catching a fish.

However, I wouldn't begin fly fishing until the early spring of 2002; there just wasn't much of a demand for fly fishing gear in Fort Worth, Texas, so getting my hands on some never presented itself. Now twenty-two years old, I was working as a plumber, and every payday I would go to either a local home improvement store and buy a new tool or go to a sporting goods store to cruise the fishing aisles looking for something I couldn't live without. Sometimes, if I didn't have bills or other expenses to pay, I would do both.

On a Friday night, prior to hitting the bar for the weekly gathering of friends to play some pool and shed our shoulders of complaints built up from the workweek, I stopped by an Academy Sporting Goods store. While roaming the fishing section, killing time, I turned a corner, and hanging there before me was a box with the words, "The Scientific Angler, Fly Fishing Combo Pack." I rubbed my eyes in disbelief, my hairs stood up on the back of my neck, and a huge smile started to creep across my face.

I looked down the aisle to make sure someone else wasn't about to steal my prize and, with hands trembling in excitement, I picked up the box. Equally as shocking was the price tag; it was only fifty dollars. I nearly ran to the checkout line and had the money out before I arrived in front of the cashier. I pulled out my cell phone and called one of my friends, telling them, "Something's come up man, I'm not going to make it out." I got in my truck and, on the drive home, called my boss to tell him something had come up and I couldn't work this particular weekend.

I got to my apartment, poured myself a drink, and unwrapped my present as though it was Christmas morning. I spent almost the entire night tying knots and getting my fly reel set up with the backing, floating line, and leader. Keep in mind this was before the YouTube era, so there weren't any videos I could watch to assist me with setting up my new toy. Luckily, the box came with some decent information; it also came with an assortment of flies to use as artificial bait.

At about 2:00 a.m. I was ready but had to wait for the sun. I went ahead and got dressed, thought about where I would go fishing, and imagined what I might catch. I looked down at my watch, and it was now 2:30 a.m. I remember thinking, "Damn sun, can't it hurry things up a bit." I tried to sleep, but my mind wouldn't let me. Finally, it was 6:00 a.m.; I got my gear loaded in the truck, headed out for some coffee, and then drove to the Trinity River. I sat on the bank, drinking my coffee, waiting for the fish to start hitting bugs on the surface. I stepped out into the shallows of the river, and just like that, I found out casting wasn't something I could just do.

I spent the entire day learning to cast. Through trial and error, I finally figured out a cast that looked okay and got the line out. I didn't catch anything though, except my ear and the middle of my back. A few weeks later I would catch my first fish on a fly rod, and though it was exhilarating it still wasn't quite the same as when I was that eleven-year-old boy.

This would be the beginning of a new journey in the fishing side of life. Through this time, I would learn that people do not go fishing just to catch fish, but for a deeper reason. I would also realize there is just something about fishing.

Through the year that followed my first catch on a fly rod, I spent at least one day every weekend somewhere on a river casting, trying to hone the skill. There are many different casts, and each has its own unique purpose. For a narrow spot among some trees, use a D-cast. When you are in a pretty tight spot with trees all around, a slingshot cast will do the trick. But if you are in a super tight spot, with trees hugging you like your mom before the first day of school, go find another spot; there are fish somewhere else on the river, I promise. When it is windy, cast with the wind, and do not ever take your eyes off the hook! Mother Nature likes to play tricks on fly fishermen and sometimes a sacrifice of blood is required. She will give a light kiss of wind at just the right moment, causing the fly to whip far behind the back, so as it starts forward it catches your ear perfectly. I am not sure how many times I have done this, but it has never been pleasant.

Getting flies, also known as artificial bait, was a bit more of a challenge. Again, I was faced with the fact that fly fishing just wasn't that big in Texas, so getting gear was proving extremely difficult. This was before the era of online shopping, and driving all the way to Oklahoma didn't exactly appeal to me. Then Tom from work said, "Try Cabela's Sporting Goods or Bass Pro Shop."

I looked at him confused and responded, "What's that?"

The sixty-nine-year-old man wearing jean overalls and a white t-shirt with his grey hair whisking like flames from under his hard hat smiled at me then ordered me to roll up the tools and get in the truck. I looked at my watch; it was barely 2:00 p.m. and the workday was supposed to end at 5:00 p.m. But it clearly wasn't up for discussion. I got in Tom's truck, another thing that wasn't a suggestion, and he put in an old Dolly Parton cassette tape. I couldn't help but laugh at how excited this old man was getting over a sporting goods store.

We turned onto a street, and I couldn't help but notice the name, Bass Pro Drive. "It has its own street?" I remember thinking. Then we pulled into the parking lot, and my eyes widened. "Wow," I muttered through an exhaling breath. There was an assortment of large fishing boats for sale, all through the lot, and the structure before me must have been where Santa Claus vacationed. We parked the vehicle and Tom and I both were out of the truck in a flash. We walked inside; it was a toy store for outdoor folks. I was overwhelmed; I gave Tom a big hug like he had just gifted me the store. Then he said, "Don't thank me, you'll never have any extra money again."

Inside the store were Bass boats, a whole house-sized section for hunting, another for fishing, and upstairs a section specifically for fly fishing. If you have never been to a Bass Pro Shop, stop reading this, find the one nearest you, and go. You can hug me later. "Thanks Tom, you were right about not having money, but thanks."

About a year later, work started to become more stressful. I was now leading my own large projects, and the expectations were high. I would still carve out at least half a day on Sundays to drive to one of the tributaries, known as forks, of the Trinity River and do some fishing. I would fill a backpack with my box of flies, a couple of bottles of water or a thermos of coffee depending on the season, a pack of cigarettes, and a six pack of beer. After affixing my reel to my rod and threading the eyelets with the fishing line, I would look at what type of bug seemed to be dominating the sky, then find a fly pattern that matched and attach it to my line. Placing my special fishing hat on my head I would light up a cigarette, open a beer, throw on my backpack, turn toward the fork, and begin strolling along the bank up stream until I came to a spot I liked; normally the first spot I saw after finishing the beer and cigarette.

If the water wasn't too deep or cold, and the situation dictated it necessary, I would walk out into the water in order to facilitate a good cast. During one of these times, it occurred to me that I hadn't caught anything in weeks; yet there I stood casting a fly I had no intention of changing in a spot I had no intention of leaving. If I was honest with myself, I had no desire to truly catch anything. It was then I stopped, looked around and realized that all this time I thought I was here trying to catch the big one when, in reality, it was nature trying to catch me. I sat down on the bank, opened another beer, and just listened to water running over the rocks, the birds chirping, and the crickets playing their tune. I took a deep breath and let it out. Something happened just then: the stress eased, and everything seemed to balance. I sat on the bank until dusk, then moseyed back to my truck. I remember sleeping significantly well that night. This became a ritual for me much as church is for other people; I could clear my mind of the week and reset for the one following. Sometimes I was more determined to catch something, and normally I did, but even if I didn't my intent was to get out, spend some time with the mother of us all, and heal the wounds left from the whip of work.

Through the next few years, I told my boss I could work until noon on Sunday only if I was truly needed. Otherwise, I had other commitments. Every Sunday, by noon, I would head out; sometimes I would catch something while half in a daze, and while always welcome it was no longer a requirement. Now I would just listen to the whispers in the wind we are often too busy to hear and appreciate that there is just something about fishing.

As I became more talented in the industrial plumbing world, the pressure placed on my shoulders increased. Soon Sunday afternoons and evenings were the only time I had for myself. If the weather was decent, I would set up my fishing rig and head somewhere close by and spend some time on a river or a creek just trying to reset. I became more of a fair-weather fisherman, and my pursuit of the sound of a ripple began to fade.

In the winter of 2007, I chose to walk a different path and joined the United States Army. So, what I didn't give away, went into storage. I packed one small backpack, hopped in a cab, and headed to my recruiter who would take me to the Military Entrance Processing Station, or MEPS, in Dallas, for shipment to Fort Benning, Georgia. For the next sixteen weeks, I trained as an infantry mortarman before being sent to my first duty station. In just sixteen weeks, the drill sergeants were able to turn a twenty-seven-year-old man into a newborn soldier. The transformation that takes place in such a short time is truly remarkable. Though, with 231 years of experience at the time of my acceptance into the infantry, I suppose they had pretty well figured out how to turn a soft-skinned civilian into an armed warrior.

In the summer, I arrived at Fort Drum, New York, home of the 10th Mountain Division. While I spent the next few years in northern New York, between training and deployments, there weren't many opportunities for fishing, which was indeed a shame because Fort Drum is very well known for its outdoor activities. The next six-and-a-half-years were much the same. Between changing duty stations, deployments, military schools, and training cadets at West Point, I didn't have a lot of time left to pursue fishing.

A soldier must suffer many hardships during training to survive in combat, but those hardships aren't endured alone. So, while my weekends were normally free, I would spend them gallivanting around the towns with my newly found brethren instead of finding a fishing hole to help me unwind. It is my firm belief there is no greater bond than the bond forged in suffering, and the greater suffering, the stronger the bond.

A new fascination had piqued my interest while in the Army: the art of fly tying. In the military, much of my downtime was spent on YouTube watching videos about fly casting, different places to fly fish, and videos of people catching giant fish. As anyone who has done any amount of YouTube surfing knows, YouTube will lure you into Alice's rabbit hole using your searches and views to keep you entranced like a snake charmer's flute. While captured in one of these spells, I stumbled upon fly tying. I had known about the craft before but had never really given it much thought due to the task's perceived difficulty and the lack of mentors. However, with the invention of YouTube, it became quite clear that it wasn't complicated at all. The more videos I watched, the more convinced I became that this would be the next endeavor in my fishing journey. Even when I wasn't watching videos, I was dreaming about the different flies I would tie and the white whales I would catch because of my not yet demonstrated talent.

At the end of six-and-a-half-years, I decided to say farewell to the Army and head back to Texas. I enlisted in the Texas National Guard to complete my eight-year requirement, so I couldn't be recalled. Now in my mid-thirties, the memory of time spent on the water, the sound of the cast, and the feel of the hook set, filled my dreams. Of course, the fish I would soon catch because of my fly-tying skill, that I still hadn't begun to learn, often kept my mind racing, preventing me from sleeping.

Not a month after my return to Texas, I received my first fly tying kit. For one hundred dollars, I bought a vice for holding the bare hook, an assortment of different type hooks, a decent array of fly-tying materials like deer hair, several different types of feathers, and about five or six thread spools. Also included was a nice little DVD that showed the basics of getting started. The DVD gave instructions on how to use the different tools like the whip finisher and how to tie the basic fly patterns like a wooly booger, mayflies, and nymphs.

Without hesitation, I arranged my station, poured a glass of whiskey, and set out to learn this fantastic skill. A week later, I finally crafted a fly that didn't have glue or material blocking the eyelet and looked close to what I wanted it to. "This might catch a fish," I thought.

By the end of two weeks, I had the hang of it and made a good variety of flies. I hadn't ventured off into my own creations, though; I was merely replicating that which I could find on YouTube.

Sometimes, when I put my flies to the test, I would get lucky and hook into a little bass; but mostly, I was catching bluegill, perch, or panfish. Even these small fish were enjoyable on a fly rod due to the rod's light structure, and I was just happy to be out on the water, attempting to put the trials of the military in the past. After a few months, I now had a pretty good grasp of fly pattern construction and began experimenting with my own creations. I would come up with an idea, think about it most of the day while at work, and then when I got home, sit at my fly-tying desk with a drink in hand to figure out how to construct the image I had in my mind. The first thing I tied was a winged black ant pattern because they are often seen flying around Texas at certain times of the year. Next was a small bluegill pattern, a favorite food of larger fish like bass. My first attempt didn't turn out so great, but after a few days or weeks of fiddling with the design and construction, I finally produced a couple I thought a bass might like. I headed to a few familiar streams, and sure enough, I was successful and caught some fish on my personally designed patterns, mostly large bluegill, large panfish, and even a catfish, to my surprise. I still didn't catch any large black bass, though.

However, I had hope that I was on the right track; I just had to find a productive honey-hole and have the right fly on hand. With this in mind, I began to craft artificial bait that mimicked the insects I frequently saw filling the sky and around riverbanks during the different seasons. One night while sitting next to the pool outside my apartment, I saw a slew of what I only know as Texas dragonflies, large prehistoric-looking things with two sets of wings, a large head filled with eyes, and a body about an inch or so long. I jumped up, went to my desk, and began construction. It took two or three days, but I finally got it. Like the others, the pattern proved successful with the common fish found in the Texas waters, but it also led to more largemouth bass catches as well. So, it became a pattern I continued to refine.

While in the military I had regressed to just pursuing the catch and not paying as much attention to the beauty around me. I do remember a few fleeting moments, generally at sunset, when I would remember to take a look around and just breathe. Usually, that was about when my phone would vibrate, and I would be called to a social gathering of some sort, or a member of my family would need help with something. After all, I was still a plumber, but now, thanks to my time in the military, I was also a general problem solver. Of course, I would stop what I was doing to render any aid that I could. Also, while away, somehow, I had forgotten that there was more to life than work, and the something about fishing I had learned to love was now lost.

At this point I had been out of the Army for about a year. I had an apartment, a job, and an overall relatively good life going, but still, something was missing. I couldn't put a finger on it, but something just wasn't quite right. Often, while trying to figure out what had me so unsettled, I would pour a drink, sit down at my fly-tying desk and tie up a few patterns, hoping it was just boredom or idle hands. If I had the day off, I would grab my fly rig, look at a map on my phone, and set out to a nearby creek to see if today would be the day I caught my white whale.

While some elements of my outings were the same, like finding a place to park, grabbing my gear, and making my way down to the water, my loadout had changed. It now consisted of my fly rod, my hat, a box of flies, and of course, my phone. If I didn't catch anything within a couple of hours, or my phone went off due to a message or a call, I would wrap it up and head back to civilization. I usually did catch something, but it was always something small that left me unfulfilled.

One night I was out with some friends, or rather friends of

friends, and the topic of fishing came up. Many in the conversation focused on not understanding how someone could spend all day fishing, hoping to get lucky. Others who were fishermen tried to defend the attacks with pictures of giants they had wrangled out of the water, using a fishing pole that cost several hundred dollars, from a boat that sat in their driveway 80 percent of the year.

My father always told me the best time to make a case in a conversation like this is after everyone else had already spoken; doing this allows you to have all the information needed to make a comment that is difficult to refute. Using my father's tactic, I waited and, when all the shots had been fired, took a sip of my whiskey and a long pull off a cigar before offering my opinion on the matter.

"Gentlemen," I began, as I exhaled the smoke from my lungs, "not a single one of you have understood what fishing is or why those of us that engage in the craft do so." I looked at the faces around me, and my opening had worked; they were now all listening so intently, their drinks were still, and, for those of you who understand body language, their feet were pointing directly at me. I continued, "Fishing is not spending all day on the water aimlessly casting into an abyss, hoping luck is on our side that day. No, it is looking at the things around you that tell where the fish might be. Watching for birds hitting a certain part of the water feeding off of baitfish. Or, looking for breaks in a current that may house a predator waiting for their prey. Or still, it might be something as obvious as fish hitting bugs resting on the surface. Regardless, it is not just blind luck." I paused, took another sip to let the sting settle a bit, then began on the second part.

"I think that you," I said, addressing the fishermen now, "have missed the real reason why we fish. It isn't the pursuit of the great whale lurking in the deep. No, it's allowing Mother Nature to heal our emotional wounds, and let us, for a moment, return to being a kid whose only worry is a dry hook or a hot Dr. Pepper." I took one last breath and ended with, "We might not all be anglers sitting on the water, but we are all fishermen with a secret place we go to recenter."

About halfway through those remarks, I realized I was no longer speaking to them; hell, I was no longer the one speaking. Something deep inside had risen to the surface and took over my voice box. That twenty-something-year-old had come out and had to say aloud what I was apparently too thick to hear internally. The night went on without much more said about the topic, but the person who needed to listen to those words did, and after that night, things began to change.

The very next day, I got up, grabbed my gear, and headed out. Over breakfast at a nearby IHOP I thought about where I wanted to go. Not looking at the map on my phone I just thought of the places I knew and decided to go to one I remembered had an excellent walkable bank and was away from anyone else. When I got to the spot, I filled a backpack with a few Dr. Peppers, a bottle of water, a pack of cigarettes, and two beers. Then I threw on my hat, grabbed my rod, tossed my phone in the glovebox, and headed upstream. I won't tell you I caught a beast because I didn't. I won't tell you I reset or found myself on that trip because I didn't. I can tell you that the thing I missed, I found. It was now only a matter of time.

Two or three months later, I was out driving around near a fork of the Trinity River, trying to find a good place to park, with the intent of walking the fork's bank quietly, hoping to sneak up on some wildlife. The area was right behind a neighborhood, but on either side of the creek was about two or three hundred meters of woods and floodplain. After about half an hour of driving around, I began to get restless sitting in the confines of my truck. I saw a driveway with some cars parked in it and looked at my watch; it was now 10:00 a.m., "Hopefully, they aren't late sleepers," I thought. I parked my vehicle on the street, walked up, and rang the doorbell.

I could hear a couple of small dogs barking and an unknown man yelling at them to calm down. I had my fly-fishing hat on, and when he opened the door, I introduced myself, "Sir, I am Michael

McGarrey; I have been driving around for about half an hour looking for a way down to the creek to do some fishing. Do you know of a spot I can park and get access?"

He was an older gentleman, probably close to eighty, clean shaven with a fresh crew cut, and thick eyeglasses. He introduced himself as Rick Dunn and began to tell me how there used to be all sorts of places to park before all the "damn Yankees" moved in. We had chatted for about fifteen minutes when he said, "Leave your truck right there, and you can go through my backyard. Fish as long as you want, I am not going anywhere today, just stop on your way out and let me know how you did."

"Thank you, sir; I'll do that," I replied.

I went to grab my pack, with my now standard packing list, and turned off my phone but put it in my pocket. I had learned to do this for the sake of taking pictures when I did catch something. I went through an entrance in the fence beside the house and traversed the backyard to an exit on the other side. This opened up to a slight hill leading down to the floodplain. I strolled along a large game trail, among the trees, listening to the sounds of birds and squirrels.

I finally arrived at the creek bank. It was only about shin to thigh deep in most places, with deeper pools scattered throughout. It had a few soft bends slowing the current down enough that the water passing over a set of rocks had a light sound of a ripple. It was now close to noon, and the sun was high, but the trees were tall pecans, about ten feet from the water's edge, with large reaching limbs that shaded the area nicely. I walked upstream and found a lovely fallen tree that offered a perfect workbench for assembling my fly rod. The sun's rays danced through the woods and reflected off the wings of a few birds in hot pursuit of a meal. The scene was so pleasant, I opened a beer, sat on the log, and watched nature do its thing. I finished up, put the empty beer bottle in my pack, and walked upstream a bit more. I finally came to a place on the bank where the Trinity River Authority engineers had put a rock embankment to prevent further erosion. It had everything a fish could want: rocks to hide behind, shade to keep the water cool, and a bend to slow down any bugs floating on the surface. I looked around and decided a nice ant pattern would do well, so I pulled one from my hat, fixed it to my line, moved to the upstream side of the bend, and began fishing.

The first couple of casts were just to get the line out and figure out what kind of form I would need to use in this area. It wasn't exactly tight, but not wide open either. I finally felt like I had the right combination sorted out and focused more on the fly's presentation. For me, the scene couldn't be more perfect. I had a cast I was comfortable enough with, meaning I didn't need to be too cautious about it. I had a fly pattern precisely for a situation like this and a spot that seemed like it should hold some fish. All that being said, I was still not tunnel-visioned on catching something; my head was on a swivel watching the world around me. In fact, on the other side of the bank was a pair of squirrels racing around the trees, and unknown to them was a hawk on my side about twenty meters away waiting for one of them to get a little too far away from the safety of the trees.

After a few minutes, I returned to paying attention to what I was doing and made a more purposeful cast, causing my ant to land softly on the surface, in the perfect spot of the current to have it pass near a rock in the water away from me. A breeze blew lightly on my neck causing the hairs to stand as if Mother Nature had just whispered in my ear that I had better pay attention. Then with a soft roll, a mouth barely broke the water's surface, causing an effect similar to water rushing down a drain. My line began to tighten and, half in shock, I almost forgot what to do. I pulled on the excess line and lifted my rod tip, setting the hook in the creature's mouth. The line raced away! I had no choice but to let it run; my leader was only a three-pound test strength, and the animal was pulling harder than ten-pounds, or so it felt!

It sped like a race car downstream using the current as its friend! This was a smart bastard, which meant it was old, which in turn translated to big. I couldn't contain myself, I looked for my audience, and the hawk was watching closely. I yelled at the bird, "Are you seeing this shit!" The beast on my line turned drastically and headed back toward me. Then with great enthusiasm it broke through the surface! Instantly, I was that eleven-year-old boy again. "HOLY SHIT!" I yelled. My focus tightened, and the words from my past came rushing back. "It only counts as a catch if you land it," I shouted as though explaining to the hawk the rules. "And these days, a person must have pictures for proof."

The fight went on, back and forth up the creek the whale raced, leaping from the water trying to throw my hook. I kept the tension ever so light, not wanting to snap my line but also not loose enough to allow the fish his freedom. Sweat began running down my brow, my forearm was now beginning to throb, but the bass showed no signs of tiring.

After what seemed to be half an hour — but was only ten minutes — the beast began to relent. A few minutes more, and I was pulling my net from my belt loop, preparing to secure the water buffalo of a fish. Holding the rod and line together in my left hand, I raised the tip high while squatting down with the net in my right hand to scoop up my prize. I pulled my white whale from the net, stood there, once again holding my trophy with my chest extending far in front of me. Smiling before the only audience I needed: the hawk and Mother Nature.

I pulled my phone from my pocket and took a couple of pictures for proof when I told the story over drinks later. They weren't great because my arms were shaking from a mixture of fatigue and adrenaline. I pulled the hook from the mouth of my catch and held the fish out to admire it. I knew that this was the moment I had been longing for since that hot summer day back in 1991. I gently placed the fish back in the water and let the current rush through its gills until it regained its strength and swam off. I remember taking my fly rod apart and seeing the hawk looking at me as though to call me a complete asshole for not donating the fish to him before flying off. I pulled my last beer of the two I had from my pack, lit up a cigarette, and headed back to my truck.

I took the walk back nice and slow, looking at the world around me as I strolled silently thinking of the fish I had just caught, enjoying the environment that had allowed me the experience. The Budweiser seemed to taste a little better and the cigarette also seemed slightly more enjoyable. I was in a state of euphoria.

After stowing my gear, I went to ring Rick's door again. He opened it up and asked, "Did you catch anything?" Removing the hat from my head and wiping the sweat from my brow I responded, "Boy, I sure did."

He smiled and said, "Good, there is a little bar up the road, follow me there. You can buy me a drink and tell me all about it."

So, over the next few hours and a few drinks I told him about the fish I had caught and how I came to understand that we don't really fish to catch fish. He and I talked about the philosophical side of fishing and in the end, we both agreed that *there is just something about fishing.*

CHAPTER 2

THE STAR-SPANGLED BANNER

I was hired by Geep Mechanical in 1999, and little did I know I wasn't just hired to a company but instead had entered what would be a six-year university. Everyone at Geep Mechanical was at least twenty years older than me.

The first few years at Geep Mechanical were probably when I acquired some of the most critical education a boy can receive on his path to becoming a man. These lessons can't be taught in a classroom or by reading a book; no, this education can only be conducted in the "real world" by professors at the school of character building. Two of the main courses taught at this university were The Art of Laughing at Yourself and Identifying when Someone is Messing with Your Head.

At Geep Mechanical, there were many instructors of these courses, and because I was the only student at this particular university, I received everyone's undivided attention. I did, however, have three instructors who gave me special attention daily.

First was Mike Callan, the Operations Director and Plumbing Supervisor. Mike taught me what was expected of an employee and made sure to follow through with punishments and rewards. One thing about Mike Callan was he could be a real asshole, but he was a consistent asshole. What I mean by this was that he was the nicest guy on the planet unless you pissed him off, and he was consistent about what pissed him off. So don't do those things, and you will be fine.

Second was Old Man Tom, who was my direct line foreman. Tom made sure I was taught things like the importance of being to work on time and helped to thicken my metaphorical skin. Tom was sixty-four when I met him at the age of eighteen. His very first words to me were, "I am too old to be training a new greenhorn. You're either going to quit or die." For the first few years, it seemed he was trying to make me quit by attempting to kill me. He even gifted me my first nickname, "Zero." Let's just say it wasn't a compliment.

Last was Len Monger, a guy from a completely different department who often worked on the same job sites with me. Len took it upon himself to teach me pretty much everything else. Those lessons began my very first day at Geep Mechanical and continued long after I left.

When I started at Geep Mechanical, I was hired as a plumber's helper; back then, you didn't have to be an apprentice to work toward a journeyman license. I was fresh out of high school and didn't know the first thing about the construction world. On my first day, Mike Callan decided to put me with Len and his partner Don who were actually part of the air duct installation department. He chose to do this so he could call Tom and inform him he was getting a new helper. This was information Tom wouldn't be happy to hear. That day Len gave me my first taste of what was in store for my future at Geep Mechanical.

On the morning of my first day, I was sitting in Mike Callan's office, when he called Len in from the hall.

"Len, will you come in here for a second," Mike Callan called out.

Len stepped into the office, "What's up, Mike?" Len said.

"Meet our new guy, Michael McGarrey. Think y'all can use him while I give Tom the good news," Mike said plainly.

"I would love to hear that conversation," Len returned with a laugh. "Sure, we can use him." Then Len looked at me. "This is Don," Len pointed to a guy in the hall as I stood up to be introduced, "go out and help him load up the van."

"Yes, sir," I replied sharply and began to follow Don out to the shop.

Don and I stopped in the breakroom on the way, "Do you drink coffee?" Don asked.

"Yes, sir," I responded.

"You don't have to call me, sir, but I get it. Grab yourself a cup. It's not great, but at least it's free," Don said. So, I did, and we continued on out to the shop.

"How old are you?" Don asked.

"Eighteen, sir," I replied.

"Cool. Did you just graduate?" Don asked further.

"Yes, sir. About two months ago," I answered.

"Well, I had better warn you about Len," Don began, "He is an awesome guy, but he is on some sort of medication for mental issues. However, if he forgot to take his meds, he can get unpredictable. Last time he threw a guy off a roof."

I laughed a little bit and said, "Yeah, sure."

But Don didn't laugh. He just looked at me stone cold and said, "No, really."

Len was six-foot-two-inches tall and easily weighed 250 pounds. And thanks to a lifetime of cutting thick sheet metal with tin snips, he had forearms like Popeye. He had a large belly from years of drinking beer and an underlying sleep apnea issue. His back was hunched from all the years of lifting things that were probably too heavy, and he had a lazy eye. The skin on his face and arms was tanned and weathered, and while at work, he always wore a baseball cap, a maroon t-shirt, blue jeans, and lace-up boots.

I, on the other hand, only stood about five-foot-eight on a good day and weighed a mere 140 pounds at the time. It wasn't hard for me to do some quick math and layman physics to determine that if

Len wanted to throw me off a roof, not only could he do it, but I would probably land on the moon.

Don and I finished loading up the van, and Len came out.

"All set?" Len asked.

"Yep," Don replied.

"What do you like to go by?" Len asked me.

"Mike is fine," I replied.

"Nope, already have one of those; choose something else," Len said.

"Um, Michael, I guess," I replied.

"Okay, Mikey, it is," Len said. "Hop in."

"Nah, I can drive; Don told me where it was," I responded.

"Nonsense. Save your gas. You can ride in the middle with us," Len ordered.

I think it is important to point out that gas was only eighty-six cents a gallon at the time in Fort Worth and where we were going was less than ten miles from the shop. But I wasn't going to argue.

The company vehicle was your typical construction van: white with the maroon Geep Mechanical logo, company phone number, and address on the sides. The van only had a front cab, and the back was bare except for an assortment of tools and materials. Because of this, my seat was between Len and Don on a five-gallon bucket.

I sat down on the bucket with my coffee in hand. Len asked me the usual questions. How old was I? When had I graduated? What jobs did I have before this one? And, more importantly, what high school I graduated from? This turned out to be in my favor because Len and I had graduated from the same high school, just a lifetime apart. So, then we talked about some high school football for the remaining ten minutes of the drive. Everything seemed pretty okay. "I guess he took his meds this morning," I thought to myself.

We arrived at the job site and began unloading tools and material. We put all the hand tools in the bucket I had previously been sitting on and moved them over to the wall of the building. The building was a one-story commercial property already in use.

"Here, Mikey, take this rope and come with me up to the roof," Len said.

I took the rope and followed Len, not thinking anything was out of the ordinary.

Then Don walked by me and whispered, "Watch out, I don't think he took his meds."

After we got on the roof, Len and I walked to the edge to pull up the tool bucket and materials. I was following Len when he began to mumble — "Why is he so close? He shouldn't be so close..." — before twitching his head and neck like a crackhead tweaking out.

Naturally, I made sure to keep my distance and never took my eyes off Len. Of course, this made it pretty challenging to be of much help or get anything done. Len continued this behavior the rest of the day. Once he even put his big, meaty hand on my shoulder, and I nearly jumped off the roof myself. Finally, it was time to head back to the shop. While Len was telling the customer we were done, Don and I loaded the tools and the parts we replaced into the back of the van. It was at this time Don bestowed a task upon me for the ride home.

"Clearly, Len forgot to take his medication this morning, and he refuses to let me drive back to the shop. Now, Len tends to fall asleep while driving, especially this late in the day. Normally I can slap him in the shoulder to wake him up, but you're riding in the middle so that responsibility falls on you," Don said.

"Are you kidding me?" I asked, genuinely concerned, looking at Don trying to get a read on whether he was messing with me or not.

"Not at all. Len will run us right off a bridge if you don't keep an eye on him," Don urged.

"What kind of hell is this?" I thought to myself, trying to wrap my head around this responsibility.

Len stayed awake at first, but things started to fall apart once we got on the freeway. He would start to drift onto the shoulder of the highway, and then his head would drop. Panicking I elbowed him in the ribs to bring him back to some form of consciousness. This was repeated several times, and a few of the times, Len actually yelled at me, "Stop that!"

We finally arrived back at the shop, and I made a beeline for Mike Callan's office, "Sir, I don't think I can work with Len anymore," I said.

"Oh really? Your first day and already telling me who you can and can't work with?" Mike said. "Tell me, Michael, why can't you work with Len?"

"Because, sir," I began, "the guy is crazy! And not just a little crazy but batshit crazy! Look, maybe Len is okay when he remembers to take his medication, but today he didn't, and I swear I think he would have killed me twice. Once intentionally by almost throwing me off the roof, and then again unintentionally by nearly falling asleep while driving on the freeway."

Mike instantly started laughing, and I knew right then I had been the target of an elaborate prank.

"Len, will you come in here for a second?" Mike called out into the hall.

Len entered Mike's office and said, "What's up, Mike?" His shit-eating grin stretched from ear to ear.

"Stop fucking with the new guy. He doesn't know any better yet," Mike directed.

"Sure, thing Mike," Len said sarcastically. Then Len walked out of Mike's office laughing.

Mike Callan then turned to me and said, "He isn't going to stop. It's probably best to assume, for the foreseeable future, that if Don starts a conversation with you, it's because he is setting you up for one of Len's schemes."

That was my very first day at Geep Mechanical. As you can see, there wasn't any mercy for my naivety. In my defense, it was my first day, and I had no reason not to believe Don. I hadn't been trained to know when someone was messing with me. On top of that, Len and Don were professionals in the art of straight-faced bullshit.

Over the years, many more situations like that would occur. But as much as Len messed with me, he also looked out for me. It was perfectly acceptable for Len or another one of Geep Mechanical's professors to teach me a lesson. But no one else outside the company had better try. He also took me under his wing outside of work, introduced me to the world of Texas music, and invited me to events where the fact that I was under the age of twenty-one was conveniently overlooked. He helped me to develop my own quick wit and always reminded me that I was still new to the game of messing with people and hadn't entirely paid all my dues yet. It didn't take long before I began to see Len as more of an uncle than anything else. I have many stories of Len, but one of them stands out most of all.

In late July of 2001, Tom, Len, Don, and I were all working on a project together in a suburb of Fort Worth called White Settlement. I had been with Geep Mechanical for about two years, and the chip on my shoulder I had graduated high school with had been whittled down to a splinter. Although, to this day, Tom can still turn that splinter into a sequoia tree with just one or two words.

At this point, I had received my second nickname, Gump, which was given to me by a group of my most beloved instructors, Len, Tom, and our female plumber Mary. We were on another job site prior to the White Settlement project, gathered around the plan table at the end of the day when Len asked, "Hey, who does, Zero look like?" I stood there, petrified to hear what responses might follow.

After a few minutes of everyone just staring at me, Len finally blurted, "Forrest Gump! He looks like Tom Hanks from Forrest Gump!"

Everyone began to laugh, hell even I began to laugh. Then Tom added, "Yeah, he is about as smart as Forrest Gump, too." I then stopped laughing.

From then on, my nickname was Gump. I wasn't too upset about it, though; it was a big step up from Zero.

Around 9:00 a.m. on this late July morning, Len, Don and I were taking a break at the White Settlement job. We always took a morning break on this job to purchase our morning poison from the food truck we dubbed the Roach Coach. Sitting in the back of Len's van, like we always did, we had begun talking about the Star-Spangled Banner and the different people who had sung it at sporting events including the Roseanne Barr version. All of a sudden, Don asked me, "Okay, Gump, you sing the Star-Spangled Banner."

"Hell no! Len has ordered me never to sing. Not even in the shower," I replied quickly.

"That's true. I have and trust me; I have single-handedly saved the world," Len said.

"Okay, then say the words to the national anthem," Don countered.

"I can't say it; I can only sing it," I responded, trying to navigate my way out of this obvious trap.

"You don't know the words do you?" Len chimed in, halfway yelling.

"I know them; I just can't remember them at the moment. It's one of those songs you need the music in order to sing along," I pleaded, but I knew I had just stepped into Len's snare.

"What?" Len exclaimed. "You can't remember them! What are you a damn communist?"

"No, damn it! I just can't remember the words. You've put me on the spot, and now I am like a damn deer in the headlights!" I yelled.

"Bullshit, you're a damn commie! Otherwise, you'd have those words tattooed on your soul!" Len bellowed.

"Oh yeah, then you sing it!" I fired back, certain that I had just saved myself from the gallows.

"No way! I am not helping a damn communist learn our beloved anthem!" Len returned.

About this time, Old Man Tom stepped out of his truck and walked past us, headed back into the job site.

"Hey Tom, did you know Gump doesn't know the national anthem?" Len yelled.

"Are you serious?" Tom replied to Len.

"What, are you a damn communist?" Tom then said to me, "I don't want a commie working on my job-site! You're fired!"

"Tom, I am not a damn communist! I just can't remember the words!" I exclaimed.

"Sounds like something a communist spy would say. Don't you think so, Tom?" Len chimed in.

"Yeah, I am commie spy, sent here to gather intelligence on the American construction worker and their drinking habits," I shouted at Len.

"Nope, I knew something wasn't right about you. What's a Latin speaking, piano playing, twenty-year-old doing working as a plumber? You have commie spy written all over you. Get off my job site before I get my gun and kill my first Ruskie!" Tom yelled.

I stood there perplexed at what had transpired in the last ten minutes. They all were so emphatic I began to question my own patriotism. Was I a commie, and didn't know it?

"Tom, I am not a communist," I tried once more.

"Get off this property, Michael, or should I say Mikhail," Tom ordered.

I walked to my truck, got in, and drove out of the parking lot headed to the shop. I was so confused. Surely, this is just one of Len's pranks. I pulled out my brand-new Motorola flip phone and called Mike Callan.

"Hey, Gump. Want to work this weekend?" Mike asked when he answered the phone.

"Um, sure? But Tom just fired me." I responded.

"What? Why?" Mike asked.

"Well, basically, because I didn't know the words to the national anthem," I stated. I was expecting Mike to tell me Tom and Len were just messing with me again and to go back to work.

"What, you don't know the words to the Star-Spangled Banner? What are you, a damn communist?" Mike shouted.

"What?" I yelled. "Did Tom already talk to you?"

"No, but Tom is right. We don't want any communists on the

payroll. This is a proud patriotic company. You are fired! You can come to get your final check tomorrow after 3:30 p.m., as usual. Just be glad I am not calling the F.B.I," he said, then hung up.

I was so confused. What the hell was going on? They can't really fire me for this, can they? I was so twisted that up I missed my exit. Hell, I missed the next three exits. How was I going to explain this to my friends and family? Were they going to think I was a communist spy, too?

Finally, I snapped out of it. "This is bullshit. It has to be a prank. Fuck it, I got booze at the apartment. I'll get a call in a few telling me it's a joke," I said to myself. I caught an exit and made my way home.

It took me thirty minutes to get home and still no phone call. So, I poured myself three-fingers of Jim Beam over some ice, sat on my couch, and called my friend, Sam.

"What's up, man?" Sam answered.

"A lot, actually. I've been fired," I responded.

"What? Why?" Sam asked.

"I'll tell you later. Wanna go out and have some drinks when you get off work?" I asked.

"Sure thing, it will probably be four o'clock before I get off," Sam replied.

"That's cool. Will you come by and get me? I'll be good and drunk by then, considering I am already having a bourbon, and it's not even noon," I said.

"Sure thing. See you then." Sam said, then hung up.

Sam finally showed up at my apartment around 5:30 p.m., and I told him about the events that had taken place earlier.

"Dude, this has to be a prank. No one gets fired for that kind of shit," Sam said.

"That's what I thought, but I haven't had a phone call saying otherwise. So, as of now, I have been fired for not knowing the Star-Spangled Banner," I said.

Then Sam looked up at me from the drink he had poured himself and said, "I gotta ask, man. Are you a commie spy?"

He laughed, I laughed, and then I threw my boot at him.

Sam and I left to go play pool at a local pool hall where we knew all the waitresses and the bartenders, which meant we were able to drink, too. It also helped that at the time, I was dating one of the bartenders, and when she heard my story, I got to drink for free. Sam and I played some pool and laughed about other events that were going on in our lives. For a little while, I forgot about my day. Around midnight, Sam had to call it a night because he had to go to work in the morning, unlike me. At home, I couldn't go to sleep, so I grabbed a bottle of Jack Daniels from my well-stocked bar and headed to the swimming pool. I drank for a few more hours, then went back to my apartment and passed out on my couch. I woke up about 1:00 p.m. and looked at my phone. Still no call. "I guess I really am fired," I thought. Then decided to get cleaned up and head to Geep Mechanical.

When I arrived a little after 3:30 p.m., I saw that Tom's truck and Len's van were already there. Since it was payday everyone else's vehicles were there, too. I parked my vehicle and headed toward the offices through the shop. As I walked through the shop, Mary and Termite, the dedicated shop guy, glared at me as though they were looking at the devil.

"I guess they got the news that I am a communist spy from Russia," I said to myself.

As I walked into the offices, half the Service Department was standing in the hall. When they saw me, they damn near knocked me over trying to get out of the offices and into the shop. It reminded me of a scene from an old western when everyone knows there is going to be a shoot-out, and they want to get out of the line of fire.

I turned into Mike Callan's office and saw Tom and Len were already sitting there.

"Should I close the door?" I asked Mike.

"No, I don't think that's necessary; everyone already knows what you are," he replied.

"You really had us fooled, Mr. McGarrey," Len said.

"If that's his real name," Tom added.

My heart crumbled. Len had never called me by my name before. I was so used to being called nicknames that being called by my actual name hurt my feelings more than being called Zero.

"We're going to follow you out so we can make sure you don't steal anything," Mike said.

Then they all rose from their chairs. I walked out the door and shuffled down the hallway toward the shop. My head was hung low, my heart was in my boots, and it was taking everything I had not to burst out in tears and beg for my job. I was so ashamed that I didn't know the Star-Spangled Banner. I still couldn't believe this was happening.

We passed through the breezeway between the offices and the shop. I opened the shop door and saw the big roll-up door was closed.

"HAPPY BIRTHDAY GUMP!" everyone shouted.

There were three coolers full of beer, and everyone had a beer in their hands. I almost had a heart attack. My knees buckled, I collapsed to the floor, and I began to shed a few tears. I had completely forgotten about it being my birthday. Len, Tom, Mike, and Don had all done such an excellent job of getting me worked up about being fired; it didn't even cross my mind. Sam, who worked for Len's brother at an electrical company was also at the shop. Len covered that base, too, making sure Sam, didn't mention my birthday while throwing in a jab about being a communist.

After Len stopped laughing, he handed me a beer and said, "Happy birthday, Gump. Meet me at my apartment tonight, and we will go out and celebrate."

"No, problem. It will take until this evening for my heart to settle anyway," I replied.

Mike informed me that Len had set the whole plan in motion a few weeks before when he found out my birthday was the day after his.

I turned to Mike and asked, "So, I still have a job, right?"

"Jesus, Gump. Yes, you still have a job. I would ask you to work this weekend, but Len has already informed me that's not going to happen," Mike responded.

After about an hour, everyone finished their beers and before leaving they each handed me a five-dollar bill to buy a drink with later.

It's like Mike Callan had told me on my very first day: "If Don starts a conversation with you, it's because he is setting you up for one of Len's schemes."

After this, Len and I would almost always get together on our birthdays, usually, at a bar of Len's choosing. At 11:59 p.m. on August 6th, I would buy two shots of Crown Royal, give him one and wish him a happy birthday. Then at 12:01 a.m. on August 7th, Len would buy two shots of Crown Royal, give me one, and wish me a happy birthday.

Len would continue to be a mentor long after we both left Geep Mechanical. More importantly, Len was instrumental in making me understand that one of the critical keys to not only surviving life but enjoying life is being able to laugh at yourself. Granted, he taught me this lesson by making me the target of most of his jokes and pranks, but to be fair, I was an easy target.

———

For Len Monger, so that he might live forever.
Borden Leonard "Len" Monger
August 6, 1955 – May 22, 2012

CHAPTER 3

09-11-2001 AND THE DAYS THAT FOLLOWED

Tuesday, September 11, 2001, began like any other day. I woke up about 5:00 a.m., got dressed, drove my truck to a nearby gas station, and bought a cup of coffee and twenty dollars' worth of fuel. After pumping my gas, I headed to the job site we had been working on for about a week.

I arrived at the job site about 6:30 a.m., walked over to Tom's truck, and informed him I would be late the next day, September 12, because the 11th was both of my sisters' birthdays. My oldest sister was born on September 11, 1963, and my other sister on September 11, 1964. My family created a big event for this every year. The whole family would get together at a restaurant called Pappadeaux's. I was particularly excited about this year because a month prior, I had turned twenty-one and could now drink legally.

The project we had been working on was for a large financial group in Arlington, Texas, which is about halfway between Fort Worth and Dallas. I had been working as a plumber for a while and had become pretty talented when it came to soldering and brazing copper. However, just because I was Geep's go-to-guy for copper didn't keep Tom from riding my ass or messing with my head. But thanks to spending more time with Len Monger, I had learned to fight back a little.

The first thing that Tuesday morning, Tom had tasked me with running ¾-inch copper water lines to some HVAC units called Variable Air Volume boxes, or VAV boxes. I distinctly remember asking, "So, Tom, what does a VAV box do, and how do they work?"

"Does knowing what they do get them hooked up quicker? No, it doesn't. Now quit stalling and go hook them up," Tom fired back.

"I get it. You don't know either," I replied.

Tom looked up from his tool bag and threw a large crescent wrench at me, which luckily barely missed my head.

"Damn, Tom. Is your eyesight finally going? It's not like you to miss," I said with a laugh. I then took off running before things escalated. He wouldn't miss a second time. To this day, I still don't know what a VAV box does.

For this project, we were turning an existing building into a large data processing center that would house several thousand computer servers. So, we were equipping the building with larger chillers to keep the area cool and safeguard it against power outages caused by Texas storms. Even though the job was indoors, the lingering 105-degree days crept in through the walls and ceiling, turning the place into a poorly lit sauna. Often when returning from lunch, we referred to the structure as "the dungeon."

There were well over one hundred VAV boxes for me to hook up with copper. When Tom came by at 7:50 a.m., I lay on my back atop some scaffolding, soldering my third box. I remember hot solder dripping off the pipe onto my arms and face. I felt like a modern-day Michelangelo, and this was my Sistine Chapel.

"Get down from there, Gump, and meet me at the truck!" Tom ordered.

"Be there in a minute, Tom. I just want to finish these last couple of solder joints," I replied, without turning off my howling acetylene torch.

"Damn it, Mikey, now!" Tom barked.

I turned off my torch and immediately scurried down the scaffolding. Tom never called me by my actual name.

"What the hell did I do now?" I thought to myself.

I caught up to Tom and followed close behind him. I didn't speak a word because I was still trying to figure out what I might have done.

Tom pulled his keys from the pocket of his well-faded overalls and said, "Get in, Mikey. Callan called and said a plane had hit the World Trade Center."

"What? How big of a plane?" I asked.

"A large passenger plane," Tom answered.

I looked to the east and said, "That's impossible; we would see the smoke from here."

"What?" Tom said.

"Dallas isn't that far. We would see the smoke from here," I said, pointing to the east.

"Jesus, Mikey, for a smart kid, you sure are a dumb ass sometimes. Not that World Trade Center, the Twin Towers in New York," Tom replied, shaking his head.

"Wait, what?" I asked, moderately confused.

Tom got into the driver's seat, and I hopped into the passenger side. Tom turned on the radio and tuned it to the news channel just in time to hear the announcer say, "Another plane has hit the second tower."

"What the hell, Tom? Do you think two planes could hit both towers by accident?" I asked Tom.

"Come on, Mikey, you're not really that naive, are you?" Tom asked as he looked at me. His eyes were aflame with anger.

"No, but no one is dumb enough to attack America, especially the mainland. And who the hell targets civilians?" I asked.

I rolled down my window, pulled out my cigarettes, and asked Tom if I could smoke with a gesture. Tom nodded, giving me permission, then said, "Yeah, not even the Japs were dumb enough to target civilians. Maybe it is a freak accident."

We talked about it being a drunk air controller and other possibilities, but then the news report said a third plane had hit the Pentagon. Tom and I looked at each other, and we knew America was under attack. I looked at the clock on Tom's dashboard. It was 8:30 a.m. in Texas.

Tom and I listened intently to the news reporter rattling off the events as he was seeing them. I sat there only hearing about half of what was being said because I was in shock and trying to understand what was happening. Tom was talking about the probability of more planes and a possible ground attack. The FAA had grounded all commercial flights and ordered all flights to land at the nearest available airports.

A report was released that at least one of the planes had departed from Boston. I leapt from the truck to call my father because I knew one of my sisters had flown out of Boston to come to Fort Worth for her birthday.

"Dad, It's Michael. Have you heard from sis?" I asked.

"Yes, she landed about an hour ago. Are you able to see this?" said my father.

"No, sir. But Tom and I are listening to it on the radio," I replied. "What is happening, Dad?"

"We're under attack, son. I guess you're getting to experience this the same way we all had to experience the attack on Pearl Harbor in '41," said my father.

"Mikey, get in here!" Tom called out from inside the truck.

I jumped back into the passenger seat with my dad still on the phone. The reporter was saying that people were leaping from the upper floors of the Twin Towers.

"I am going to let you go now, Michael. Call a little later," said my father.

"Yes, sir. I will." I replied, and my father hung up the phone.

"How bad does it have to be for someone to jump from thirteen hundred feet, Tom?" I asked.

"Pretty damn bad, Mikey. Pretty damn bad," Tom said softly. I had never heard softness in the old man's voice before, which added gravity to this moment.

Tom and I continued to listen. Tom began to tell me how this reminded him of sitting on his parent's living room floor listening to the radio as reporters were talking about Pearl Harbor being attacked. Tom and my father were relatively close in age. Tom was older by about five years.

Then things went from bad to worse. The reporter called out over the radio that the first Tower had collapsed. I again looked at the clock on Tom's dashboard. It was now 9:00 a.m. in Texas. A few minutes later, another report informed us that a fourth hijacked plane, Flight 93, had crashed somewhere in Pennsylvania. I remember Tom saying, "That thing didn't crash; it was shot down."

Tom and I sat speechlessly. Then at 9:50 a.m., the news station cut to a reporter in Manhattan, "The second Tower has fallen! The Twin Towers are gone!" The announcer let out a fearful cry. Then the reporter let out a defeated sigh. The broadcast announcer and the reporter continued to talk about all the people who were still in the building and all the firefighters and first responders who didn't make it out. I don't think he knew he was still on the air as he began to sob. All Tom and I could do was just sit there and stare at the radio. Neither of us said a word.

It was at this moment I truly understood what it was to be an American. I was angry that anyone had the nerve to attack the United States of America. And even though the attack was fifteen hundred miles away, it felt as though it was right down the street. Those New Yorkers I used to talk so much crap about, especially during the current baseball season, were no longer a bunch of Yankees. They were now neighbors, friends, and family. I was saddened by the lives lost and mourned them as though I knew them personally. I also wanted vengeance, and only blood would satisfy that want.

Sometime after the Towers fell, Mike Callan came to the job site. He gathered all of us together and said, "Y'all go home and be with your families and friends. I will call you tonight and let you know when we will be returning to work. Clay, will you lead us in a prayer?"

Clay Turner nodded his head and said, "Let us pray. Lord, give our leaders the strength and wisdom of David so we might find those responsible. When they are found, send Archangel Michael to watch over our soldiers as they seek to bring them to justice. And when that justice is done, may you have mercy on their souls. In Jesus's name, we pray. Amen."

I made the sign of the cross because I am a Catholic, then we all shook hands and went our separate ways.

As I pulled out of the parking lot in my truck, I took my cell phone from my glove box and called my buddy, Sam. He and I agreed to meet up at a bar called the Oui Lounge to watch the rest of the day with other Americans we both knew well.

The Oui Lounge was a bar established in 1952 by two men looking to make a little extra income. They bought the building, turned it into a bar, and hired a French girl to operate it. Hence the name Oui, because that's apparently all she ever said. After a few years of nagging from their wives, the gentlemen sold the bar to a familiar acquaintance. He kept it open from that point forward. It remained the Oui Lounge until 2013. It is still there, and a bar, just operating under another name.

The Oui Lounge had an old wooden front door, but most regulars parked in the back, so their wives couldn't see their cars, and would come in the metal back door. The front wall consisted of full-size windows that stretched the length of the front of the establishment. The windows, however, had dark shades to cover them, so no matter what time of day it was, the Oui was always as dark as night.

My father had been going to the Oui since it opened, and when my siblings and I were old enough to drink, we made sure it didn't run out of rent money. I became such a frequent flier that when everyone had to leave at closing time, I was allowed to stay and help clean. I would pick up glasses and wash them; my only payment was a few more martinis and a ride home.

The Oui had a cigarette machine next to the front door, two pool tables, and three tube televisions. The Oui was split into three areas with wooden wall dividers. The front bar area had two televisions and a pool table. The bar room pool table was where all the better players would gamble so the bartenders could control the bets. The middle room was a lounge that was full of tables and chairs. There was also a jukebox and a dance floor. The back room was what I called the Rowdy Room where most of the younger, poorly mannered college kids hung out. It also had a pool table and a television. While there was a bar, it wasn't used to serve drinks anymore. Another thing to know is that in 2001 it was still okay to smoke in bars. So, for the last fifty years, people had been smoking in the Oui, and it smelled like it, and if you spent more than five minutes there, you would, too.

When I walked in the front door on September 11, 2001, everyone was in the Rowdy Room watching the television, even the bartender, Trent. Everyone was smoking, so there was a thick cloud of smoke between my head and the ceiling.

I approached the bartender and said, "Hey, Trent. Can I get a whiskey on the rocks?"

"Sure, Michael. You know where it is; serve yourself. I trust you," Trent replied.

I went back to the bar and began making myself a drink. I watched the front television as I scooped the ice into my glass. I poured myself a double, and Sam walked in the backdoor as I put the whiskey down. So, I pulled another whiskey glass and poured him the same without asking.

"Are you moonlighting here now?" Sam joked.

"Yeah, but everyone can only have whiskey," I said.

"That works for me," Sam replied.

I handed Sam his drink, and we went to the back room.

"Hey, Trent, I went ahead and made Sam a drink, too. We will settle up later," I said.

"No problem, Michael," Trent replied.

"Hey, Sam," Trent said as he held out his hand.

"Hello, Trent," Sam returned, and he shook Trent's hand.

Not much else was said. We continued to watch television. At the Pentagon, the firefighters were going full blast fighting the jet fuel that was still burning. In New York, first responders were trying to get accountability of those who had escaped to get an accurate count of those who were still trapped. I looked at my watch, and it was now 10:30 a.m. in Texas. At about 1:30 p.m., Sam and I decided to leave. We went up to the bar to settle up with Trent, but when he saw we had only had two each, he said, "Don't worry about it, guys. We have all had a pretty tough day."

"Thanks, Trent. We will see you Friday as usual," I said.

Sam and I walked out the back door into the blindingly bright sun of mid-afternoon.

"You're more than welcome to come over to the apartment and watch the news," I said to Sam while trying to let my eyes adjust to the sunlight.

"No. Think I'll go over to my mom's for a bit," Sam replied.

"Okay, I'll see you Friday then. Damn it, I parked in front," I said.

"Yeah, I'll see you Friday," Sam returned.

Sam got in his truck, and I walked back through the Oui and out the front door to my truck and drove home. When I got to my apartment, I put on a pot of water to boil so I could make some pasta for dinner. Then I took a shower while I waited for the water to boil. Once my pasta and meat sauce were ready, I poured a glass of iced tea, sat on my couch, and continued to watch the news. I had just finished my dinner when Mike Callan called.

"Hello, sir," I answered.

"Hello, Mikey. How are you holding up?" Mike asked.

"Not sure, to be honest, sir. I am still trying to make sense of it all. I get pissed off because I don't know if I should scream, hit something, or cry," I replied.

"Yeah, Mikey, I get it. Well, be back in Arlington on Thursday. We are giving everyone tomorrow off with pay," he said.

"Yes, sir. I'll see you Thursday then," I replied.

"Yeah, and Mikey, I am not trying to freak you out, but they might implement the draft over this," Mike said cautiously.

"Yes, sir, a few older guys at the Oui said the same thing," I replied.

"Okay, well, talk to you on Thursday then," Mike said and ended the call.

I remember being up well into Wednesday morning watching the news. But for the life of me, even up to the present day, I can't remember if I ever wished my sisters happy birthday.

On Wednesday afternoon, I went over to my parents' house to visit for about an hour. We watched the news as search and rescue teams dug through the rubble of the Pentagon and World Trade Center, looking for survivors. At this point, it was still unclear if Flight 93, which had gone down in Pennsylvania, had been shot down, or if the passengers had regained control and forced the plane to crash. My father and I both believed it had been shot down but that the government would claim the passengers had forced it down. However, it came out the following week or so that the passengers had learned the Capitol building or the White House were the intended targets. Knowing this information, several passengers used cell phones to call their loved ones to say some last goodbyes, then rose up against the attackers long enough to force the plane down.

Every time I think of Flight 93, I get goosebumps. I stick my chest out a little prouder as an American. I get goosebumps because of the immense amount of courage it must have taken to follow through with an action that wasn't just going to end your life but the lives of everyone on board. I am also indescribably proud because it gave those asshole terrorists their first taste of how far Americans were willing to go to win a fight. At that moment, a spark of American badassery was relit, and a damn bonfire of true patriotism raged hotter than the surface of the sun.

My mother, father, and I were sitting in my parents' bedroom watching the television. My father and I were sipping iced tea with lemon and mint, and my mom had a glass of ice water. My mother was more distraught than my father and me because she grew up on Long Island, New York, and hadn't moved to Texas until she was eighteen. She still had quite a bit of family in New York, and everyone was apparently okay. However, my mother still had a solid connection to the city.

I stayed at my parents' house until my butt began to hurt from sitting on the floor, then stood up and said, "Well, I am going to go up to the Oui for a bit."

"Okay, Michael. We're going to stay here," my father replied.

I got in my truck and began the eight-minute drive to the Oui. I don't think I had seen, or have seen since, that many American Flags on so many houses, cars, and children's bicycles in all my life. I walked into the backdoor of the Oui at about 3:00 p.m., and, once again, Trent was bartending.

Trent was a tall six-foot-three-inch man with a long brown beard who always wore a straw cowboy hat that had to have been older than I was. Imagine if Charlie Daniels and a grizzly bear had a son, and that's what Trent looked like. He was highly intelligent, often having conversations with my dad about physics and levels of math that would interest Einstein. Trent was always kind and well-tempered, even when he had to physically escort someone from the bar. He told me that what determines whether someone wins a fight or loses a fight is how that person enters the fight. Luckily, I was never escorted out.

I approached the bar, pulled a two-dollar bill from my wallet, and handed it to Trent, asking, "Can I get coins for the cigarette machine and a Bacardi and Coke with a lime?"

"Yeah, sure thing," Trent replied.

Trent came back and handed me two Susan B. Anthony dollars

and said he would make my drink while I got my cigarettes. I made my way along the bar to the front toward the cigarette machine, stopping and saying hello to all the regulars, many of whom had known me since I was in diapers.

After returning to my drink with a fresh pack of Marlboro's, I asked Trent, "Have they found anyone else?"

"No, not yet," he answered.

I spent the next couple of hours at the Oui talking to Trent about the job site in Arlington and trying to decompress from everything that had happened in the last thirty-something hours. We all sat there and watched the television somewhat quietly, except when the search and rescue teams would pull someone out alive. Then the whole bar went up in a roar like our favorite sports team had just scored. We all got shots and tossed a couple of more bucks into the FDNY donation jar. I left the Oui about 5:00 p.m. for my apartment to watch a little more news until I finally went to sleep.

Thursday morning, I got to Arlington a little earlier than usual, about 6:15 a.m. Of course, Tom was already there and, to my surprise, so was Len. Len was leaning up against the hood of Tom's truck on the driver's side. So, I went around to the passenger side and leaned on the door, and said through the open window, "Hello, gentlemen."

Tom and Len both nodded in acknowledgment, and Tom turned down the radio, so it was loud enough to hear but easy to talk over. Thursday the 13th was also the day the FAA lifted the flight restrictions on commercial flights.

I was confused by Len's presence, so I asked, "What are you doing here, Len?"

"Mike sent me out to help set those diesel tanks, and so he only had to make one stop to drop off checks later," Len answered.

"Right, I forgot about the tanks. What time is the crane supposed to be here, Tom?" I asked.

"About eight o'clock, Gump. Why, do you have somewhere else you plan to be?" Tom inquired.

"No, sir," I said with a smile.

A little before 7:00 a.m., Tom, Len, and I started to head into the Dungeon to start the day. We were joined by Clay Turner.

Clay Turner, to me, was quite a colorful character. He was drafted during the Vietnam War but, to my knowledge, never made it overseas. He exited the Army with an honorable discharge, but — according to a story he told me — just barely. Apparently, toward the end of his military career he and another soldier were guarding a rocket silo somewhere in the United States. Clay was the senior enlisted of the two and decided they needed some beer to help the night pass quicker. The only problem was neither of them had a vehicle. That didn't stop Clay, though; he found a Jeep nearby and decided it wouldn't be missed. It turned out that the Jeep belonged to a colonel, and when Clay returned with a case of beer, the colonel was at the silo waiting. Needless to say, that didn't go over too well. Now that story might be complete bullshit, but then I could also see a young twenty-year-old Clay pulling that stunt.

After the Army, Clay worked as a welder and became a deacon at a church in Oklahoma. However, when I knew Clay, he had left that position for his own personal reasons. At the time of September 11, 2001, Clay was about fifty years old, and because he was a welder, always wore a Wrangler pearl snap shirt, blue jeans, and slip-on steel-toe boots. Clay's shoulders were so broad the man couldn't snap the top three buttons on his shirts. Clay might have been the most naturally strong person I have ever known. Clay still lived in Oklahoma and made the four-hour commute to the Fort Worth and Dallas metroplex every morning in a company vehicle because that was how valuable he was to the company.

About 8:00 a.m. on September 13, Clay, Tom, Len, and I were working outside, getting ready to start setting the two large diesel tanks with a crane. These diesel tanks were about as wide as a single-car garage but long enough to hold two cars end-to-end. As we got the rigging ready to hook up to the crane, we heard a loud explosion. Everyone ducked and ran for the nearest cover. I was hot on Clay's heels because he and I had been working together. I looked up, and everyone had drawn a pistol from somewhere. Everyone except me. Once again, I felt a little naive. The explosion turned out to be an electrical transformer that had blown on a power line a couple of a hundred yards away. When we knew it was all clear, everyone who had a weapon returned it to their holsters and we continued crane operations.

As we were about to set the first tank, Len came over to Clay and me to lend a hand on our corner and asked Clay, "You think they will bring back the draft?"

"Yeah, I imagine they'll have to once they determine who's going to receive our wrath," Clay answered.

"When do you think, they will start sending out notices?" I asked Clay.

"They probably already have; they just haven't arrived yet," Clay replied.

"Are you ready to go if you get yours?" Len asked me.

"I don't know, to be honest. But I'll go anyway," I responded. "Hell, if they don't send me one, then I'll probably just join."

"You're twenty-one years old with two brothers that are too old to draft. You'll definitely get one," Clay added with confidence.

With that, we finished setting the tanks, and not another word was mentioned about a potential draft. But that didn't stop me from thinking about it. It wasn't until I was headed out to lunch that Tom asked me, "You okay, Gump? You look stressed."

"Yeah, I am okay, Tom. You really think they'll bring back the draft?" I asked.

"Oh, yeah, most likely. I guess that would have me pretty nervous, too," Tom said. Then he got in his truck, turned on the radio, put his seat back, and took a nap.

When I returned to the Dungeon after lunch, I went back to work hooking up copper lines to the VAV boxes. At about 2:30 p.m., I was outside getting some air and saw Mike Callan pull in the parking lot. He talked to Tom for a bit, handed him checks, then left. I went back in to continue working. About an hour later, Tom came over and told me to tell everyone to start rolling up and come to his truck for checks. Tom always had me perform the task of walking around the more prominent job sites telling everyone when it was time to get ready to leave. By the time I spread the word, picked up my own equipment, and headed out to Tom's truck, it was 4:50 p.m. I walked out the large roll-up door and could see everyone already gathered around the bed of Tom's truck. The three of them just looked at me as I approached.

"What is it? What did I do now?" I asked with a nervous smile.

"Here's your check, Gump," Tom said.

"Thanks, Tom?" I replied.

"Mikey, your dad dropped this off at the office. Mike Callan thought it would be best if I gave it to you," Len said.

I held in my hand an envelope from the U.S. government. The envelope was neatly typed and had my parent's address.

"Told ya," Clay said.

"It's probably nothing, Gump. Open it," Len added.

I opened the envelope, and there in print was a set of draft orders. The orders instructed me to report to the Dallas Military Entrance Processing Station on Monday, September 17, 2001, at 7:00 a.m.

"Yep, it's draft orders. I will report on Monday," I said out loud.

"That sucks, Mikey. It was nice working with you," Clay said as he handed me a cigarette.

My hands were shaking so badly I could barely get the damn thing lit.

"Well, I'll see some of you tomorrow," Clay said, then walked off toward his truck.

Len and Tom shook my hand, then Tom said, "Go ahead and take tomorrow off, Gump. I'll call Mike Callan and tell him about the letter."

"Watch yourself over there, Mikey," Len said. Then Len and Tom got in their vehicles and drove off.

By the time I walked fifty feet to my truck, I had finished the cigarette Clay had given me and was lighting another as I climbed in my driver's seat. I pulled my cell phone from my center console and called my father.

"Hey, dad," I said with a shaky voice.

"Hello, Michael. What's wrong?" Dad asked.

"I got the letter you dropped off at Geep. It's draft orders. I will report to Dallas on Monday morning," I said, letting out a deep sigh.

"What letter? I didn't drop off a letter. And there's not a damn draft. The news would have announced that by now," said my father.

"Wait, what?" I yelled. "You didn't get a letter from the government and take it to Geep?"

"No. First, there is no way the government could get draft notices out this quickly. Secondly, I would have just called you and told you to come by the house when you got off work. I think someone is messing with you again, Michael," my father said as he began to laugh.

"I am going to kill them! They were all in on it!" I yelled. I was extremely pissed off, but I was also laughing hysterically. "Okay, dad, thanks. I need to go burn some houses down now. I'll talk to you this weekend," I said.

"Okay, son. Just remember it's only illegal if you get caught," my dad said, then he hung up.

I started up my truck and called Tom as I was pulling out of the parking lot in Arlington.

"Hey, Gump," Tom laughed as he answered the phone.

"Y'all are some real assholes, you know that?" I yelled, laughing as well.

"Yep, we know. We had to get out of there quickly because the look on your face was about to make us lose it," Tom said. "Well, I'll see you tomorrow bright and early," Tom said, then he ended the call.

The next day, which was Friday, September 14, 2001, everyone filled me in on the little prank. Clay had somehow gotten a copy of his old draft orders to Len on Wednesday. Len then had one of his friends change the information to match my name, the current dates, and recent events. Len then typed up an envelope that I now know looks nothing like a government letter and placed the orders inside. Tom was filled in on the little plan Thursday morning and was more than happy to play along. Mike Callan, however, didn't know anything about the scheme, that's why Tom offered to call him for me.

After everything was explained, I remember saying, "You know one day I am going to snap and take an ax to all of you."

"Why do you think we all keep guns in our vehicles, Gump?" Tom laughed, wiping a tear from his eye.

"Oh, Gump, don't take it so hard. Come by Woody's tonight, and I'll buy you a couple of drinks," Len said.

"Like hell, you'll buy all night! That shit had me fucked up," I replied.

Then we all went into the Dungeon, Tom went back to riding my ass, and I got back to work installing VAV boxes. For me, thanks to that little prank, things began settling into what would be the new version of normal. However, anytime a plane seemed to be flying too low, everyone noticed.

———

In Memory of 09-11-2001
May we never forget the events of that tragic day.
May we never forget that, at least for a while, we were all proud flag-waving Americans.

CHAPTER 4

THE BUILDING BLUNDER

I turned twenty-two in the summer of 2002 and had been plumbing for Geep Mechanical, which is pronounced Jeep, for a little over three years. I had started working at Geep right out of high school and was easily twenty-five to thirty years younger than the youngest person there, so most of the Geep personnel thought of me as a nephew. Because of this, in those three years, I had learned a lot about life and a little about plumbing. During those years I also earned the trust of my company by becoming a reliable employee and a capable plumber.

By the middle of May, there was a good set of Texas storms pushing through Fort Worth, which many of us Fort Worthians knew might be the last bit of rain we would see until October, so many were happy to see the rain. Most of the plumbers took time off because no one liked working around the shop on those days mainly because they didn't like the busy work or the fact that the supervisors always wanted to come out and harass anyone that might be working in the shop. I didn't mind, though, for two reasons. First, busy work never bothered me; I would sweep the shop floor for eight hours until the concrete was worn smooth. Secondly, I was a twenty-two-year-old with bills. I couldn't miss a day's work unless there just wasn't anything I could do about it, like if the weather was excellent and I wanted to go fishing. Everyone knows you don't take a sick day when you're sick; you take a sick day when there's something you would rather do than work.

One particular Wednesday around midmorning I was paged over the shop intercom. "Mikey, please see Mike Callan in his office," the secretary and accountant, Miss Diane, called out. It could be one of two things: either Mike was sending me to the house because the floor was clean enough, or I was getting sent to one of the food plants to look at something that had to be repaired during shutdown hours.

I hung up the broom and made my way through the short corridor that separated the office from the shop. The office was merely a large four-bedroom, two-bathroom house that had been converted into a set of offices with a small break room. They added a large two-story shop area to the north of the offices. They also fenced in a large parking area for all the construction equipment and a pipe yard to the north of the shop. The office and shop sat on a corner lot that backed up to a railroad to the west.

When I arrived at Mike's office, the door was open, and I could see Miss Diane was sitting in there talking with Mike. I removed my hat and waited in the hall until Mike acknowledged me, "Come in, Mikey, and have a seat."

Miss Diane stood and, as she walked out, said quietly with a smile, "Don't worry, you're not in trouble."

"How long have you been working here now, Mikey?" Mike asked as he sat in front of me, looking at his pencil. I knew he only did this when he already knew the answer to the question he had asked.

"A little over three years now, sir," I said confidently, knowing it was getting close to four years.

"I think it's time to see just how much you've learned." He said as he looked up to his desk where a set of blueprints lay. "Take these out to the shop and figure out what you're going to need. Pull as much of it from the shop as possible. I'll answer any questions you might have, Mikey. I know it's small but take your time with it," he finished.

"Yes, sir," I responded excitedly. I grabbed up the prints and headed out of his office quickly as though the decision I knew he had thought hard about might somehow be reversed.

The reason for this project was more than just to see how I did flying solo. The real point was to see if I was ready to go to Austin to take the Texas State Plumbing Exam. In the time I had worked for Geep, I had not only accrued the hours I needed for the exam but, more importantly, the knowledge of codes and the installation experience. Still, if Geep was going to pay for me to go down and take the three-day exam, they wanted to be damn sure I would pass.

I walked back out to the shop and sat at the break table just past the corridor from the offices. The only other person in the shop was a man named Termite, who was sitting at the break table reading the newspaper. To be clear, Termite was his nickname. He was the dedicated shop guy, and we called him Termite because the man was a wizard when it came to carpentry. I call him Termite here because I can't remember his real name for the life of me.

"Wow, they gave me my own job," I said to Termite.

"That's awesome, Mike!" Termite said proudly. "You damn sure deserve it, kid. Anything you need, you just let me know."

I sat down at the shop table, unrolled the prints, grabbed a notepad, pencil, and cup of coffee, and started going through the pages. The project was small. A simple drive-thru teller bank. The whole structure was rectangular with a square main building for the tellers and two drive-thru lanes outside: one for utilizing the teller and one for the ATM. The main building was simple enough — just a bathroom with a sink, a floor drain, and, of course, a toilet. There was also a break room with a kitchen sink. For those who don't know, a plumber with three years of experience should find a project like this incredibly simple. The best part of the project wasn't how simple it was but how insanely close it was to my apartment. It was less than three miles down my street. I remember one morning freaking out because I thought I had overslept, only to remember it was just down the road, so I crawled back in bed.

After writing out my material list, I started scouring the shelves on the mezzanine for all the fittings I could find and put them into boxes that I carried to the bottom floor. I then pulled any special materials and tools I might need for this little endeavor's underground portion. The special items included things like lime chalk for marking where my ditches needed to be dug and a grade sight level for making sure my ditch had the right depth and fall. Once I had everything gathered next to the large roll-up door of the shop, I pulled my company truck into the bay, went through my list, and started checking things off before loading them. I then identified my missing pipes and fittings and called an order into a nearby plumbing supply. I also asked Termite to bring the miniature excavator to the job site when he got the opportunity. It was now nearing 3:00 p.m., so I had time to go to the supply house and make a run by the site before heading home.

I pulled up to the job site about 5:00 p.m. and began unloading all my pipe and fittings onto the dirt pad where the future parking lot would be. The form boards that would mark the outside walls of the structure weren't completely up yet, but two of them were, and that would be enough to get me started in the morning. I looked around and noticed that there wasn't a mini excavator. So, I grabbed my Nokia brick cell phone and called Termite.

"What's up, Mikey?" Termite asked as he answered my call.

"Hey, Termite, what's the story on the excavator?" I asked.

"Oh shit, man, I forgot all about it. Can I get it for you first thing tomorrow?" he questioned.

"Yeah, man, that'll be fine. It will take me an hour or two to get the ditches marked anyway; just try to get out here first thing," I offered.

"You got it, kid. See you in the morning. I'll bring donuts for my screw-up," Termite said, then hung up.

I stood in the middle of the pad, looking around to get a feel for where everything had to go. I also found the main water supply for the building because, for some reason, it wasn't shown on the plans. The job site had just become a little better. To the west, across the street, was the levy to the Trinity River. So, I walked across the street and up the levy, and the view before me was impressive. The spot in the river had a nice bend to it and was shallow to offer a good ripple, perfect for fishing. Across the river was a paved walking trail, full of college girls jogging, working on their already lovely physiques. "Maybe I should milk this for as long as I can?" I thought to myself. I turned and made my way back to my truck, got in, and drove the five minutes to my apartment. I grabbed the prints, took them inside, and unrolled them on my coffee table. I took a shower to knock the dust off from the shop, went over to my well-stocked dry bar, and made myself my usual cocktail at the time, a Bacardi and Coke with a lime. I set the drink on a coaster and scaled out the measurements to my main lines off the west and south walls. Those were the two form boards that I knew were up already. I wrote the measurements down in my notepad, then rolled up the prints and decided to head to my favorite bar for a couple of drinks.

The following day I woke up at 6:35 a.m. and was at the job site by 7:00 a.m. after stopping at the gas station for fuel and coffee. There still wasn't an excavator, but I didn't really expect there to be. However, the concrete workers were already there and would be done with the form-boards within the hour. I got out of my truck and figured I would call Termite to ensure he hadn't forgotten about me again.

"Good morning, Termite," I said when he answered. "Just making sure you hadn't forgotten the donuts you promised."

"I hadn't forgotten, bud; I am loading the trailer now and will be on my way," Termite responded.

"Okay, awesome, I will see you when you get here then." I hung up the phone, grabbed my notepad and my 100-foot tape measure, and began pulling measurements and marking them by driving wooden stakes into the ground. I then got the lime chalk and began playing connect the dots. Once I was done with that, I was ready to start digging, but there was still no excavator. I looked at my watch, and it had been just short of two hours. "What the hell, Termite?" I said to myself. I grabbed my phone from my Wrangler, pearl snap shirt pocket and once again called him.

"Termite, did you get lost?" I asked, somewhat perturbed.

"No, sorry, Mikey, Dee came out and started barking orders for things he needed right away." I could tell by his voice he felt terrible for letting me down. Dee was another supervisor of a different department. Dee and Mike Callan hated each other.

"It's okay, Termite, but I am going to have to call Mike. Sorry to throw you in the middle like this," I said.

"It's okay, bud; at this point, I kind of want you to," Termite answered back.

"All right, I will see you soon," I said as I hung up. I then called Mike Callan.

"Hello, Mikey," Mike answered. "What can I do for you?"

"Well, sir, I would like to get started digging, but apparently, Dee has more important things for Termite to do than to bring out the excavator. Termite was loading up at 7:30 this morning when I first called to remind him," I responded.

"I guess you already have your ditches marked, and all you need to do is dig?" Mike asked.

"Yes, sir," I replied.

"I'll take care of it," he said as he hung up. I swear I could hear him smile at the joy of getting into Dee's ass.

I no longer concerned myself with the excavator. I knew that Mike would have that sorted out quickly. So, I went to a coffee shop that was within walking distance.

The person behind the counter, who might have been the same age as me but looked as though he was in kindergarten, asked me, "What can I get you?"

I then laughed a little and responded, "You know the black stuff you put in a cup? No sugar, no cream. Where I come from, we call that black coffee, but I don't want to confuse you."

I must admit I was the only non-college student in the place. I got my coffee and walked out to sit on top of the levy, watching as the midmorning joggers went by and counting how many fish I saw jump. Trying to determine what type of fish they were helped pass the time. This was the same spot I learned to fly fish, mentioned in "Fly Fishing Fiasco."

It was now about 10:30 a.m.; Termite had just delivered the excavator, and I eagerly got to work digging my ditches. By the end of the day, I had dug all my trenches. I also called a local quarry to deliver a load of sand in the morning. I then called Mike Callan.

"Hey, Mikey, how's it going out there?" he asked.

"Pretty good, sir, thanks," I replied, then continued. "I have a load of sand being delivered tomorrow morning for bedding in this ditch. Any chance I can get the bobcat out here?"

"Damn, sorry Mikey, it's headed out to Duncanville," he said. "You want to get a rental?" he asked.

"No, that's not necessary. It's not that much of a ditch; I can do it with a wheelbarrow," I replied. "Just thought if the bobcat was just sitting there, I would give Termite a reason to get out of the shop."

"Yeah, I am sure that would have been appreciated," he commented. "When do you think you'll be ready for an inspection?" he finished.

"Well, if all goes according to plan, I'll be done by the end of the day tomorrow and will have everything filled with water. If it all holds, then probably Monday," I replied.

"Well, you just cursed yourself, so, I will call for one on Tuesday," he stated with a laugh. "I'll see you tomorrow afternoon when I bring out checks." Then he hung up the phone.

"Way to go, Mikey, you just talked your way into more work," I said to myself, thinking about hauling sand to the trenches with a wheelbarrow. "Oh well, you've done harder things," I thought, then I started picking up my tools and loading them in the truck. I needed to get home and get cleaned up. It was Thursday, which meant Ladies Night at the Horseman, which also meant dollar beer night.

I remember the next day well. It was the first day the temperature dial hit 100 degrees. In Texas, at least back then, it wasn't officially summer until the temperature hit 100. It also probably wouldn't drop below 100 again until late September, possibly October. I got to the job site a little before 7:00 a.m., just as the dump truck was pulling up with my load of sand. I showed the driver where to dump it and signed for the material. Then I grabbed my shovel and the wheelbarrow and got to work. It was a long day, but that just made the beer taste better when it was over. By five o'clock that afternoon, when Mike Callan showed up with my check, all the pipe was in and had been holding water well over an hour.

"Hey there, Mikey, any wet spots?" Mike asked as he handed me my check.

"No, sir, and she has been holding for well over an hour," I replied.

"Good, because I called the inspection in for Monday," he laughed. "It looks good. Nice job. Can you work tomorrow?"

"Sure. Kettle Cooked Foods?" I asked.

"Yeah, they already have enough people, really, but you know that place better than anyone else we have, so I am sure they wouldn't mind having you," he smiled. "Really, nice work here," he added as he slapped me on the shoulder and walked back to his Suburban.

Kettle Cooked Foods was a food plant where I spent many nights working. Between midnight and 4:00 a.m., I fixed leaks while they were shut down for sanitation. But I wouldn't end up working that weekend because this was the same Friday that I found my fly rod mentioned in "Something About Fishing." It worked out, though, because I would park at the job site and do a walk-through to make sure nothing was leaking on my way to the river just over the levy.

I arrived Monday morning at 6:30 a.m. to have enough time to top off any water that might have evaporated and top the air pressure off on the waterline if needed. Mike Callan arrived at 7:00 a.m. just as I was putting the hose back in my truck.

"Everything okay?" Mike Callan asked.

"Yes, sir. Just topping off the evaporation," I replied.

"Okay, inspectors never show up before eight o'clock. So, is there any place to get a cup of coffee around here?" he asked in response.

"Sure is Mike, right over there. We can walk to it from here," I said, laughing internally. I couldn't wait to see what Mike said when that punk asked him what kind of coffee he wanted.

We walked over to the coffee shop and waited in line behind the several sorority girls.

"Well, I see why you like to come here," Mike said quietly with a smile. "Wishing you had gone to college yet?"

"Nope. These girls look good but have less sense than a doorknob," I said back. "Now, if I run into one going to school for agriculture, the story might be different."

We approached, and a different guy was behind the counter, but he shared the same qualities as the first person I had encountered there.

"What can I get for you, sir?" the kid behind the counter asked.

"A medium coffee, please," Mike responded.

"We only have short, tall, or venti, sir. And what kind of coffee?"

"Do you go to college?" Mike asked.

"Yes, sir. I do," the poor kid responded proudly.

"Then I feel bad for your parents wasting their money on someone who can't figure out that if short is the smallest and venti is the largest, then tall is probably a medium," Mike began. "As far as what kind of coffee, just regular black coffee. You do serve that here, don't you? Do you want anything, Mikey?" he finished.

"Oh, no, sir, thank you. I know a girl named Noelle, who works at Snookie's Bar and Grill across the street, who gets in early to set up for lunch, she puts a pot on for me. I just didn't want to miss this exchange," I responded, barely able to contain myself.

After Mike and I left, we walked across the street to Snookie's. I called Noelle on the way and asked if it would be okay if my boss and I hung out until the inspector showed up. She said yes, and when I knocked on the door, she let us in.

"Hey there, Michael," Noelle said as she opened the door, a cup of coffee in her hand. Then she saw the cup from the coffee place in Mike Callan's hand. "Oh, Michael set you up, didn't he?"

"Yeah, he did. One day he'll learn it's not wise to pick on the boss," Mike responded. "I am Mike Callan. Thanks for letting us wait here. It's not even eight o'clock, and it's 100 degrees."

"No problem. I don't know how Michael makes it till noon out there, we need to have two pitchers of tea just for him when he comes in for lunch, or no one else will get any," Noelle responded.

I led us to a seat in the back that I had picked out from the day before and sat down. It was directly under an air conditioning vent.

"You're only here for two full days, and you already have a lunch spot where the staff knows you?" Mike asked curiously.

"Mike, I live right down the street," I replied. "I have been coming here a lot longer than just a couple of days."

"Ah, that makes more sense," he said.

At about 8:15 a.m., I saw the inspector's truck at a stoplight just down the street.

"There's the inspector, Mike," I stated.

We got up, and I waved to Noelle, thanked her for letting us in and let her know I would be in for lunch so to save my spot. We were strolling up to the job right when the inspector was pulling onto the dirt parking pad.

"Hello, sir. I am Mike Callan," Mike said, reaching out to shake hands with the inspector. "And this is Mike McGarrey, the apprentice who did all the work. He is trying to prove he is ready to go down to Austin for the exam."

I reached out my hand, "Hello, sir."

After everyone was introduced, the inspector looked over my work with a critical eye. He checked the fall of my sewer lines, measured the depth of my ditches, even let some air pressure out of my water lines to make sure the gauge held, and I didn't cheat by putting on a rigged meter. After about an hour of scrutiny, he was finally done. Then he looked at me and said, "This is some of the best damn work I have seen in years. I get probably thirty hotshots a month trying to prove they are ready to go get their license, and all of them end up getting a red tag and failing my inspection. I hope you keep up this kind of quality. I have to go back to my truck for a green tag; I really didn't expect you to pass."

We got to his truck, and he filled out the green tag and handed it to me to give to the general contractor in charge of the project. We sat and talked about how long I had been working with Geep and other stuff like fishing. Then he concluded with, "Okay, I'll let you get to work burying all this; Mr. Callan, if Mikey is going to be doing the above-ground stuff, you don't have to be here with him. I trust him." And with that, the inspector drove off.

"Nice work, Mikey," Mike said. "Go to a rental yard and get a tamper and have a bobcat delivered. I'll have Termite come get the excavator. Oh, and obviously, tie the waterline back in while you wait for the bobcat."

"Yes, sir," I responded. I had to force myself to keep my shoulders hunched.

"And Mikey, try not to take too long of a lunch today," he smiled.

I spent the rest of that day and half of the next day backfilling my ditches and tamping them. After lunch, on Tuesday, I called Mike Callan at the office and asked him where he wanted me to go next. He told me to go out to Duncanville, where Old Man Tom and the rest of the Geep Mechanical construction crews were building a ground-up food plant. I would go on to do a job in downtown Dallas and eventually got my own much more extensive job in a place called Farmer's Branch.

Right now, you're probably wondering just where the hell is the blunder? This all seems pretty awesome so far. And you're right it is. Which makes what unfolded next sincerely soul-crushing.

While I was in Farmers Branch working on a large banking

company's future data processing center, Mike Callan called. It was now close to the end of September, but it was still blistering hot. I answered the phone, thinking he probably wanted me to work on the weekend.

"Hello, Mike," I answered.

"Hey there, Mikey," he responded. "Do you still have those prints from that Fort Worth bank job?"

"Yes, sir. In my truck," I answered back.

"Great. Go dig them out and call me back," Mike returned.

"Yes, sir," I said and hung up the phone. This could only mean one thing: I had screwed up somewhere. I was going through in my head what I might have done, and the only thing I could think of was that one of my vent stub-ups had missed a wall. I got to my truck, dug out my prints, and rolled them out on the hood of my vehicle using my tape measure as a paperweight. Then I called Mike Callan back.

"Okay, sir, I got them," I said nervously when I heard him answer.

"Great!" he replied. I could hear the sarcasm in his voice. "Can you tell me, while looking at your prints, where the toilet stub-up is supposed to be?"

"Um, you mean the toilet vent?" I asked.

"Did I say the toilet vent!" Mike responded clearly, getting more agitated.

"Um, twelve inches off the back wall and twelve inches off the sidewall," I responded, somewhat confused because almost all toilet stub-ups have the exact measurements.

"Oh, so it's not supposed to be in the middle of the front fucking door?" He yelled violently through the phone. "Stop what you're doing, roll up your tools, and get your ass out here."

"Yes, sir," I responded, confused and slightly panicked.

By the time I had got my tools picked up and loaded in my truck to head to Fort Worth, it was 3:00 p.m. on a Friday. While Farmers Branch is only about thirty miles from Fort Worth, traffic on a

Friday afternoon is notoriously bad; it took me three hours to get there.

After the long and agonizing drive back to Fort Worth, I finally turned the corner onto the street the job site was on. I could instantly see the white four-inch PVC pipe standing like a proud sentinel, guarding the middle of the doorway. My heart sank. Part of me wanted to stop my truck, turn around, call Mike, and quit. But I knew that wasn't an option. I pulled into the now paved parking lot, stepped out of my truck with my prints, and could only watch as Mike Callan approached.

"Give me those prints. Mikey," he ordered.

I handed them to him, and he unrolled them on the hood of my truck and flipped to the plumbing page letters reading up. Then he ripped off the pages before the plumbing page, and there, under the staple, was the north and south arrow, pointing in the opposite direction. My heart and my ego sank. Mike Callan was just standing there fuming, waiting for me to say something.

"Well, I don't guess we can pick the building up and turn it around?" I said awkwardly, trying to play off the seriousness of this mistake. By the look on Mike Callan's face, he didn't think that nearly as funny as I did — and still do. I was waiting to hear him say I was fired, so I braced myself.

"Mikey, I don't care what you have to do, but this shit better be fixed by 8:30 a.m. tomorrow morning," he barked, then pulled out his phone to call Termite at the shop. "Termite, expect a long night hanging out at the shop. Don't leave until Mikey is sure he is done with you for the night." He mashed the end-call button, then redirected his attention to me. "8:30 a.m., Mikey. Not 8:31 a.m., 8:30," he said emphatically before driving off in his Chevy Suburban.

I took off my hat, squatted down, and buried my face in my hands. I honestly felt I was going to cry. I pulled out a cigarette and could barely get it in my mouth, not to mention light it, due to my hands shaking. At this time in my life, I didn't really smoke unless I was drinking. Still, at this point, I would try anything to calm my nerves and to procrastinate a little longer before walking inside to assess what steps needed to happen. My head was so wrapped up in how big a screw up this was I couldn't hardly think.

I walked in and looked around. I had fixed harder things in less time, but I was still in shock about the whole situation. I kept asking myself, "How the hell did the general contractor not notice this before pouring the concrete and putting up the damn walls?" While a valid point, it didn't change that the disaster lay firmly on my shoulders, and now I had to make it right. I walked back outside and looked at my watch. It was now 7:30 p.m., I had just thirteen hours to determine my fate. Then, out of the corner of my eye, I caught a glint of sun reflecting off a car's window. It was Old Man Tom pulling into the parking lot.

Old Man Tom, as I had grown to call him, respectfully, was sixty-four when I hired on to Geep. I remember when I first walked onto his job site fresh out of high school, not knowing the first thing about plumbing. The construction world was different back then. No one really gave a shit about your feelings. In fact, if you showed that you had any feelings, that just made them harass you more. Tom was no exception. The very first day Mike Callan introduced me to Tom, I reached out to shake Tom's hand, and he just looked at me and said, "I am too old to be training another greenhorn. You're either going to quit or die. I'll make sure of that."

He wasn't lying. For the next couple of years, his primary focus was trying to treat me so poorly I would quit. But my last name is McGarrey, and like any good Irishman, I am as stubborn as they come. So, I didn't quit, and eventually, I proved myself to him, and he became one of the most important mentors of my life.

When I saw Tom pull into the parking lot, I took my first breath of relief. Just having Tom's ability to organize a job site made this not seem too impossible.

"How are you doing, Mikey?" Tom asked, from inside his truck, with the window down.

"Not too good, Tom. Not sure where to begin. I can't seem to think straight," I replied.

"Mikey, you fucked up. But it's fixable. Shit, I have seen you fix bigger problems than this in four hours during a shutdown at Kettle. The only difference is they weren't your fuck ups," Tom said, then let out a long trail of chewing tobacco spit into the parking lot. "Tell me what we need from the shop, and I'll run and get it," Tom finished.

"Hell, Tom, I don't know!" I exclaimed. My voice cracked a bit with despair.

"Bull shit! You're one of the best at fixing other people's mistakes. Now stop feeling sorry for yourself and fix this one!" he ordered.

I took a deep breath and cleared my mind. Tom was right, I was feeling sorry for myself, and I had fixed more tragic mistakes than this. I pulled out my notepad and started thinking through what needed to happen and in what order, to get this done in T-10 hours.

"First thing that has to happen is I need to get that concrete removed. The most effective way to do that is with a concrete saw. So, better get the concrete saw and jackhammer from the shop. Also, some four-inch pipe fittings," I said out loud while writing it down in my notepad.

"Now we're cooking," Tom said, and he turned up his radio while I finished putting together a list of things we needed from the shop and gave him instructions to get anything we didn't have at the shop anywhere he could. The nice thing was because I was the one who put the pipe in the ground, I knew how everything was plumbed and exactly what needed to be fixed. I tore off the list and handed it to Tom. "Fly like the wind, Tom, and if you think of anything I might have missed, grab it. I would rather have it and not use it than the other way around."

As Tom was pulling away, I pulled out my phone and called a local concrete company to request ten yards of concrete for a 4:00 a.m. pour. Ten yards would be way too much, but I sure as hell didn't want to have too little. Then I grabbed my prints, a chalk-box, and a few other hand tools to start laying out where I wanted to cut the concrete. Now that I had accepted my screw-up, it was time to fix it in a way that no one would ever know, in the future, that anything had ever gone wrong. I kept thinking to myself, "I can do this. It's going to be close, but I can do this." As I completed marking out the lines where I would cut the concrete, Tom showed back up with most of the things I needed.

"Mikey, we were short a couple of fittings but, I have Termite going to a supply shop to get them," Tom stated. "What's first?"

"First is getting this concrete cut and pulled out," I said. I pulled the concrete saw and the jackhammer out of the back of Tom's truck. Then I fueled up the saw and filled its reservoir tank with water. I fired it up, started cutting, and immediately saw our first problem. The saw wasn't cutting all the way through the concrete. Our saw could cut through six inches of concrete, there was no reason the concrete should be any thicker, but it was. Well, at least a majority of it was. I continued cutting because it would still make jackhammering easier and make the pieces of concrete breakout with clean edges for when we poured the cement back. About 9:45 p.m., Termite showed up with the rest of our fittings.

"Here you go, Mikey. Need anything else?" Termite asked.

"Yeah, I don't suppose you have any lights on that truck?" I responded.

"No, but I'll sure as shit run and get some," Termite said back.

Luckily Texas is flat. So, the bit of light shining through the door and through the bank teller's window continued to give us some illumination for another forty-five minutes. I got done with the saw, and the now sixty-nine-year-old Tom grabbed the jackhammer and went to town busting up concrete. Tom worked that jackhammer like a kid on a pogo stick. I grabbed my specially made sledgehammer and went to work on the other end.

My sledgehammer had a forty-pound head and a one-inch iron stock handle. Altogether, the damn thing weighed sixty pounds. Although it was heavy and took some strength to swing, it made short work of anything you wanted to break once you got into a grove. To this day, when someone wants me to swing a sledgehammer for a workout, I barely break a sweat. My body just knows the right way to swing one with the least amount of effort.

About 10:15 p.m., I heard Tom stop jackhammering. I looked back, expecting to see Termite with the lights, and I did. But, with him, I saw two other shadows approaching: Mary, our female plumber, and Forrest, a friend from high school I had helped get hired.

"Hey, Mikey," Mary said as she carried in some construction lights with stands and started setting them up. "What can we do to help?"

"Oh, Mary, I'll take care of this; it's my screw-up. Besides, Tom is leaving in about forty minutes anyway," I responded.

"Bull shit, Mikey," Mary fired back. "Every time I have ever been in a bind and called on you, you never said no. Regardless of what time it was or if you had been on another job all day. I am not passing on the opportunity to return the favor."

"Okay, Mary," I laughed. "You don't have to stay, Forrest," turning my attention to him. "Get home to that new wife and baby of yours."

"Fuck you, Mike! First off, we have been friends since high school. Secondly, I wouldn't have this job if it weren't for you. So, I am staying, too," he stated emphatically.

"Okay then, Mary, you team up with Tom on that jackhammer. Forrest, you and I will work this sledgehammer and race to the middle," I ordered.

I remember it being like an oven inside that building. It was so humid that the walls and ceiling were sweating. The temperature outside, even at 10:40 p.m., was in the nineties. Add in the construction lights acting like heat lamps, plus four bodies going as hard as they could trying to bust concrete, and basically, you have a sauna. After the teams split up, Forrest and I had put down my trusty sledge so we could shovel some of the debris out of our portion of the ditch. We carted the debris out to the parking lot with a wheelbarrow, and when I went back inside to grab my sledge, it was gone.

"Tom, you damn klepto, give that back," I yelled with a laugh. "We still need that, Old Man!"

"Chill out, bitch!" Tom replied as he picked up the heavy beast and began to work on a piece of concrete while Mary was working the jackhammer. "You set the damn thing down so clearly you are tired. Here use this; it's more your size, pussy!" Tom finished, pulling a ball-ping hammer out of a loop of his overalls and throwing it at my head. We all busted out laughing.

"You missed, Tom, that's not like you," I returned.

"I'll kill you Monday when this is behind us," he fired back.

By 11:00 p.m., we had the concrete out, which was the hard part, really. All that was left was to dig the pipe up, rip it out, re-plumb everything, bury it back, tamp it, and replace the rebar all before 4:00 a.m. when the cement was scheduled to arrive.

"Okay, Mikey, I am all out of steam," Tom said. "Looks like you got it from here anyway."

"Yeah, Tom, I'll cut Mary and Forrest loose in about an hour or so as soon as we get this pipe dug up. Thanks for staying as long as you did. I truly can't thank you enough," I responded.

"I'll remind you of that when I have you buy my lunch one day next week," he laughed in reply. He then gathered up his tools, and we all walked with him out to the trucks. We needed a break.

"Mikey," Tom started as he climbed in his truck, "next time, find the damn arrow, will ya, please. I am getting too old for this shit." Then he drove off.

The air was still, and you could hear all the people having a good time at Snookie's just across the way. Forrest, Mary, and I all lit up cigarettes and chit-chatted about different things. I told them about my latest fly fishing adventure, Forrest told us about his new baby, and Mary told us about the latest news working in the service department. Even though Mary was a licensed plumber, she worked for Dee in the service department, not for Mike Callan. He was the plumbing and new construction supervisor. While Mike could be an asshole, at least he was consistent. Meaning you knew exactly what would set him off; as long as you didn't do those things, everything was peachy. Dee was not that way. Let's just say he liked to play politics with everything.

"Well, we might as well get back to it," I said to Mary and Forrest as our cigarettes were nearing their butts.

We walked back inside and began digging. The pipes at the deepest were only about thirty inches. So, it didn't take us long to get the line exposed. Forrest and I did most of the digging while Mary started laying out fittings. Mary, at this time, was somewhere near her fifties and not in great shape. But she wasn't afraid to get dirty, and she sure as hell taught me a lot about plumbing before this debacle and after. By midnight we had the old pipe out and had put in the new line. We checked everything four times. I measured everything, then Forrest measured everything, then Mary, then I did one more time.

"Okay, guys, y'all get out of here; I can take care of the rest," I said to Mary and Forrest.

"You, sure Mikey, that's a lot of backfilling by hand and tamping?" Mary asked.

"Yeah, we don't mind staying, man," Forrest added.

"No, I got it. I have four hours to get it backfilled and tamped before the cement gets here. I can handle that no problem," I returned confidently.

They both nodded in agreement and shuffled to their vehicles. I could tell they were worn out; I was, too. In the past five hours, we had done what I had spent two days doing. I know they would have stayed, but I also know they didn't want to, really.

"And then there was one," I remember saying to myself. I pulled off my hat and wiped my brow with my sleeve, then walked back into the ring for the final round. I spent the next three hours backfilling the ditch. While Forrest and I were digging the pipe out, we were careful to separate the dirt from the sand as best we could so I could backfill it with sand first. I covered the new pipe with about six inches of sand, then sprayed the sand with water so it would settle around the pipe. Then I filled about six to ten inches of regular dirt on top of the sand, wet it down a little bit, then fired up the tamper and compacted the hell out of the soil. I then rinsed and repeated this process until the ditch was filled to the bottom of the existing concrete. If you have never seen a tamper, imagine a large jackhammer with about an eight-inch-wide square foot on the bottom instead of a spike.

Next was replacing the rebar, which was actually the easy part of it all. I just had to drill some holes with a hammer drill and drive the rebar in with a little three-pound hammer. I was just tying my last piece of rebar when the cement truck pulled in. It was 4:00 a.m. on the dot. I got up and walked outside to greet the driver.

"Hey, man," I said as the driver stepped out of his truck.

"Hey, where's everyone else?" he responded curiously.

"I am it, man. Got a ditch in there I need to pour, the bad thing is I am wheeling it in with a wheelbarrow, so you'll have to bear with me," I responded.

"You did ask for the fast-setting mix, right? Because that's what I have," he asked.

"Yeah, I need this to be able to walk on in four hours," I answered.

"All right. I can back up to that door if that will help you out?" the driver recommended.

"Hell yeah," I responded. "I am going to get my wheelbarrow, a long two-by-four, and my cement finishing shit."

That cement driver and I had ourselves a nice little groove going. I would dump about six to ten loads then use the two-by-four to drag the cement even with the top of the existing concrete. While I did that, the driver would fill and dump about three more loads to help me out until I could take back over. It only took us about one hour and some change to get the entire thing poured and floated out smooth. By 6:00 a.m., I was shaking his hand to thank him for his help, and then I told him how I wound up in this mess in the first place. After he left, I crawled into my truck, kicked my seat back, set my alarm for 7:45 a.m., and took a nap.

When I woke up, I went inside to check on the cement. It was already hardening well enough to walk on. I had a little less than hour before Mike Callan either showed up or called. I knew I had better not just have it fixed but better than fixed. So, I drove to a Home Depot only a quarter mile away and grabbed a handful of fittings I needed to put in the sink stub-outs and the toilet flange. I also grabbed a few other fittings so I could start running the vents. I got all I needed then raced back to the job site. When Mike called, I had the sink stub-outs on, the flange set, and was just beginning the vents. It was 8:29 a.m.

"Hello, sir," I answered.

"How are we looking, Mikey?" he asked.

"We're good. The concrete is hard enough to walk on; I wouldn't drive any machinery on it for a few days, though." I replied.

"Okay, go ahead and put the stub-outs for the sinks in and set the toilet flange," Mike said in return.

"Already done, sir," I said.

"What about the vents?" he asked.

"No, sir. I have them started, but I need to come to the shop for some pipe and a ladder," I answered.

"No, don't worry about it. You can do it Monday. Go home, lick your wounds, and I'll see you at the shop Monday morning," Mike said. "And Mikey, let's try to avoid fuck ups like this in the future."

"Yes, sir," I responded with relief, shocked that I wasn't being fired.

I caught a lot of harassment from my co-workers in the months to follow, but Mike never mentioned it again. I learned several lessons from this experience, though. The most important: anything is fixable, so long as it's not life, limb, or eyesight. Also, you should always allow someone to correct their mistakes, and when they do, forgive them completely. That doesn't mean you can't help them build a little character by bringing it up every time the opportunity arises. After I got out of the Army some thirteen years later, I met up with Oldman Tom again for a beer. He walked into the bar, set down a set of blueprints, and asked me to show him where the north and south arrow was, then had me point which way was north.

CHAPTER 5

THE FLY FISHING FIASCO

I have spent all my memorable life fishing, but my fishing dreams changed when I saw the film, "A River Runs Through It." I no longer dreamt of catching that big bass. No, instead, I dreamt of catching that great big ole' trout on a fly rod. Never had I known fishing could be such an art.

Growing up in Texas, the opportunity to fish for trout was only presented once a year in winter if the winter had been cold enough. And winters in Texas were rarely cold enough. Even more rare was an available fly rod. But as anyone who enjoys fishing knows, a bad day fishing is still a pretty good day. Even if it's not the style of fishing you would like to be doing. Little did I know the hands of fate had been listening to my dreams and were working to present me the opportunity I craved.

Around the age of fourteen, my brother's friend John Forney took me fishing on a river called the Brazos, just below the Possum Kingdom Dam. From Fort Worth, Possum Kingdom is about a two-hour drive which, even in Texas, "ain't close." I remember the trip well. We listened to "alternative music" on the way, Nirvana to be exact, which was a nice break from the classical music I was bombarded with by my father. I had brought along my spinning reel, and we stopped for minnows and some breakfast sandwiches at a bait shop near the dam.

We arrived at the Brazos just as the first glimmers of light began to crest the tall pecan trees that are plentiful along its banks. I pulled my fishing gear from John's car, and we walked to the river's edge. John had a spinning reel setup and a strange case that looked similar to something that would hold building blueprints. The water was low, and we were catching fish. But this part of the Brazos is famous for large striped bass, and those had been evading us.

After about an hour, John looked at me and, almost stealing a direct quote from "A River Runs Through It," said, "This is a good spot. You stay here. I am going downstream a bit."

"Okay, good luck! Let me know if you find those stripers," I requested.

A few hours went by, and I grew tired of fishing alone and was ready to break for lunch. I started to walk downstream, looking for John. Then as I stumbled across the large rocks along the bank and rounded a bend in the river, I saw John standing about knee-deep in the water casting a fly rod.

I stood there, shocked at what I was seeing. I felt almost betrayed. "I didn't know John was a fly fisherman," I thought to myself. "Have I not told him how much I longed to learn that craft?"

I saw him giving that magical cast and was hypnotized. I could not focus on anything else. Finally, John saw me watching in awe and asked, "Wanna try it?"

My response wasn't in the form of words but direct action. I moved instantly toward John. I practically discarded my spinning reel on the bank in disgust, almost as if I was ashamed I had ever used such a monstrosity.

He handed me the rod, gave me a few quick instructions, then turned me loose while he walked up to the car to grab our lunch. I stood there in the water swinging the rod back and forth, trying to remember everything I had seen in "A River Runs Through It" about casting. When John returned with our lunch, I went to the bank to eat. While we ate, John gave a few more pointers. After lunch, I returned to the river with the fly rod while John enjoyed the warmth of the sun and a few cold beers from the ice chest.

I never truly mastered the cast that day. Still, John, always being the enthusiast, said, "Now that you have the cast down, you have to leave the fly in the water long enough for something to eat it." Then he rested his head on a rock to take a nap because I had stolen his fly rod.

I never hooked up with the fly rod that day because I never let the fly rest on the water long enough. But casting that fly rod invigorated me with a new passion. I knew I wanted to fly fish, but again, there weren't any fly rods available at the local Payless Cashways, a hardware store near my parents' house. There weren't any Walmarts in those days, so, between Payless and the Army-Navy store, there weren't any other places my father would go for outdoor stuff.

Eight years later, while walking through an Academy Sports Center, I stumbled upon a fly rod. As mentioned in "Something About Fishing," I was over the damn moon. The extended version of my learning how to properly cast a fly rod isn't in that story. I mention it briefly where I say, "I didn't catch anything, though, except my ear and the middle of my back." Let's go further into that part of the story because it's pretty amusing.

So, I bought the fly rod and headed out to the Trinity River once I got it assembled. I parked at the construction site I was working on described in "A Building Blunder." I walked through the construction site, checked the water levels in my plumbing stub-ups, and checked the sand around the pipe in the ditches to ensure there weren't any leaks. Satisfied that everything was good and confident about the inspection on Monday, I left the site to cross over the levee and head down to the river. I took off my boots and socks, rolled up my pant legs at the water's edge, and waded into the water about shin deep, almost like I had done with John on the Brazos. I tried remembering everything he had told me on that trip, plus everything I had seen from "A River Runs Through It." YouTube hadn't been invented yet, hell cell phones were still relatively new, so my only guide to casting was a mental image of what a cast was supposed to look like.

At first, the casts were short, the fly landing only a few feet in front of me. I tried casting a little further only to have the line knock off the straw cowboy hat I was wearing. Luckily, I caught it before it floated away.

"Well, that's not going to work," I said to myself.

I walked over to the bank, laid down my fly rod in the tall grass, slipped my bare feet into my boots, then headed to my truck to exchange my cowboy hat for a ball cap and retrieve my cigarettes. When I walked back through the construction site, I saw my buddy Sam working. He was an electrician and, apparently, his company had been hired to do the installations.

"Hey, Mike. I thought that was your truck. You missed a hell of a crowd at Woody's last night. What are you doing?" Sam said.

"Oh, just on the river doing some fishing. I found a fly rod last night at Academy," I replied.

"That's why you cancelled?" Sam laughed.

"Yep. I like you, Sam, but I love fishing," I laughed with him.

Sam walked with me over to my truck, where we stood to talk a bit more.

"Have you caught anything?" Sam asked.

"Just my hat," I laughed, setting my cowboy hat upside down on my seat and grabbing my ball cap off the dash

"Do you have your phone with you?" Sam asked as he laughed also.

"Nah, if I drop another phone while fishing, Mike Callan will take it out of my flesh," I answered.

"Okay, I'll come to get you when I take lunch," Sam said as we walked back to the pad of the construction site.

"Cool, sounds good," I replied.

I made my way back to where I had left my fly rod and returned to practicing my cast. I clearly had a lot to learn about casting because things began to happen that I didn't even know were possible. On one cast, the fly's hook caught the orange float-line in mid-air. The point of it was actually hooked into the line. The line folded upon itself during another cast, landing on the water in a figure-eight. Soon I began seeing tiny dots on my leader and thought I was picking up foam from the water but, upon close inspection, saw that the leader had tied itself into knots. "How the hell did that happen?" I asked no one, utterly confused. I would learn later those are called wind knots. I began to settle on the idea that I would be on the river all day just trying to cast.

Slowly, I started to develop a decent-looking cast and began growing more confident as my casts were becoming longer. But that confidence evaporated quickly when "YOW! What the fuck!" I exclaimed. I now had a fly for an ear piercing, and the fly line was resting on my shoulder. Luckily, the hook wasn't so deep that the barb had gotten into my skin, and I was able to pull the fly out without too much discomfort. But I was now bleeding from the top of my ear. I wasn't deterred, though; I once again continued to hone the skill of casting. Only now, I was paying a hell of a lot more attention to where the fly was in my back cast.

Soon after piercing my ear, I heard someone calling my name. It was Sam. He was standing on top of the levee, waving his hand, signaling me to come to him, and tapping his wrist, letting me know it was time for lunch. I walked out of the water, wiping the sweat from my brow with the back of my forearm. I put on my socks and boots on the bank then began my trek up the steep levee.

"Come on, slowpoke. I ain't got all day. Some of us have to work," Sam called out when I was about halfway.

"Yeah, yeah," I yelled.

"Something bite you?" Sam asked when I finally reached the top.

"What?" I replied.

"Did something bite you?" he repeated. "Your ear is bleeding."

"Oh yeah. The hook on my fly did," I replied with a chuckle.

Sam began laughing so hard I nearly had to carry him down the other side of the levee. I stopped at my truck to put my fly rod away and put my cowboy hat back on. Then I asked Sam, "Where do you want to go?"

"Is Noelle working?" Sam asked, looking over at Snookie's.

I looked in the parking lot of Snookie's, then replied, "Yeah, that looks like her car."

I looked in the side mirror of my truck at my ear and cleaned the blood off with a towel I had in the back cab. Then Sam and I walked over to Snookie's.

"Hey, fellas," Noelle said as we walked in. "It's a scorcher today; y'all want a pitcher of tea?"

"Sam, might, but I'll take a mojito. If you don't mind making one? And a beer while I wait for that," I replied.

"Oh, sure, you aren't working?" she asked.

Then Sam chimed in, "No, this dumb ass is fishing while I work. But I'll take a beer also and a pitcher of tea, please."

"Fishing? Isn't it too hot?" Noelle asked.

"Yeah, if you're trying to catch something," I answered.

"You're not trying to catch something?" Noelle replied, a look of confusion on her face.

"No, someone got themselves a fly rod. Oooooohhhh," Sam said as he made jazz hands.

"So, because you have a fly rod, you're not trying to catch fish? I am really confused," Noelle said, laughing at Sam.

"Not really. I am trying to figure out the whole casting thing," I replied.

"Yeah, ask him what happened to his ear," Sam said, grabbing my ear and folding it down to show Noelle the hole in its back.

"Hey, asshole, that hurts," I laughed, nearly hitting my forehead on the chair as we approached our table.

"I can't wait to hear this. I'll be back with y'alls beers in a minute," Noelle laughed, then left to get our drinks.

I told Sam and Noelle about my ear, and Sam told us about Woody's the night before. After lunch, Sam returned to work, and I returned to the river to continue practicing after switching hats. I was highly determined to learn a proper cast. A couple of hours after returning to the river, it happened — the event that would make the day so memorable, as if it wasn't already.

So, let's paint this scene accurately: it was a hot summer's day after lunch, and I figured I should try to even out my tan. I decided to go shirtless once I had returned to the river's edge but tucked my t-shirt through my belt loop, so I had it with me if I started to burn. I took off my boots and socks and left them on the bank as I had before, then walked out a comfortable distance.

This portion of the Trinity had a nice breaking bend with a shallow ford that caused the current to ripple lightly. There were paved trails along the tops of the levies that joggers and cyclists used, and, on this day, it was quite active. There was a light breeze that made the heat of midday almost bearable. If you haven't ever been to Texas in mid-summer, let me assure you it's sweltering. Even standing in the middle of the river with a breeze, I had a nice layer of perspiration beading on my body, attempting to keep me cool. The gentle wind had the trees whispering unknown secrets, but unfortunately, they were too far from the water to offer any shade. I was again standing in the Trinity River, only wearing my jeans and ball cap, casting my fly rod to and fro.

As I began casting, I wisely kept my eye on the fly as it flew behind me in the back cast. But as I continued to get better casts, my confidence grew, and my wisdom was replaced with complacency. I stopped paying attention to the fly when it was behind me and was now only watching how it landed on the water's surface, hoping for that perfect presentation. Hours passed, and soon I was able to get the fly to land so softly on the water it barely caused a ripple, but no fish were biting because it was too damn hot. I was confident that if I could keep presenting my fly this way that when the sun began to set and the water started to cool, the fish would become active, and maybe then I might catch my first fish on a fly rod. Unfortunately, sunset would not be until 9:00 p.m., and fate had other plans in store for my day.

Like any good mother, Mother Nature never fails to remind us of important life lessons. So, when the mother of us all saw I no longer focused my fly because I was becoming a little too cocky, she reminded me of the dangers of complacency. I remember the lesson well even today as I sit here writing.

I was casting pretty well at this point and had lovely long casts laying out nicely in front of me. Because I was getting better, the hopes of catching a fish began to creep into my mind as the sun inched closer to fading behind the trees. The one-hundred-plus-degree heat was no longer a concern, so maybe what happened next was not only a lesson but also Mother Nature's way of telling me to get the hell off the water before I died of a heat stroke.

I was casting my line to see how far out I could get it, and Mother Nature saw her opportunity. A light breeze blew across my bare chest in the middle of one of my back casts, and I remember thinking momentarily how nice it felt. I even tossed up a "thank you" to Mother Nature. I think she must have laughed a little when she heard my thank you because before I could return my thoughts to the cast, I screamed, "YOW!"

The light breeze had drifted my fly perfectly behind me so that when it came forward, it caught me, hook first, right in the middle of my back. Of course, Mother Nature's aim was perfect, and the fly hooked me right in the one part of the back I couldn't reach. I tried, trust me, I tried. And in all my trying, I made things worse rather than better. I just set the hook deeper into my back. I knew the barb was now under my flesh, so I did what I knew I had to do, and I cut the line. Cutting the line was also painful because I didn't want to cut the knot I had spent hours the night before tying on the end of my float line. So, I pulled the line as far as I could bear and cut the leader.

"I would rather have a complete stranger pull the hook out than Sam," I thought to myself. So, I walked across the river to the bank, up the opposite levee, and sat on a bench across the paved trail. I put my t-shirt on to not look like a complete weirdo and disassembled my fly rod. I was trying to figure out what I should do in this predicament. Sam was definitely out of the question because he would tell Len. That was the last person I wanted to be involved in this embarrassment. I also knew it wasn't something that required a trip to the hospital. So, my only hope was to get a good Samaritan on the trail to stop and help. Several joggers went by, but none would slow to my cries. I can't say I blame them, though. I was probably quite the sight, standing there barefoot, with old, faded Levi's, a white t-shirt wrinkled from being in my belt loop, and a purple, dirty old TCU ball cap. But finally, a sympathetic soul approached.

"Ma'am, I know this is odd, and I swear I am not a weirdo, but can you help me out?" I asked with as much of a puppy dog look as I could create.

With a cautious smile on her face, she responded curiously, "Sure?"

I turned around, and out of the bottom of my shirt was a piece of fishing line, wagging in the wind like an excited dog's tail.

Before I could lift up my shirt to show her what I needed from her, she instantly started laughing. She laughed so hard, in fact, she couldn't help me because she had to sit down on the bench. She then looked up at me standing there, then looked down at the fishing line between my legs and began laughing even harder, eventually having to lay on the bench. I must admit I was starting to wish I had gone to the hospital.

After a few minutes passed, she wiped the tears from her eyes and said as controllably as she could, "Okay, let's see."

When I lifted up my shirt, she laughed a little more but then said almost sympathetically, "Wow, that looks like it hurt."

"Not near as much as my ego does right now," I said softly with a clear tone of humiliation. I opened my pocketknife and handed it to her. "If you need to cut the skin, it's okay. My knife is pretty sharp, so it shouldn't be too difficult."

"I'm afraid I need to. The barb is in there pretty good. I wish I could tell you this won't hurt, but it's going to," she said with a more serious tone. I could tell she was trying to focus on the task at hand. "Hump your back, so the skin pulls tight. It might help me see the hook under the skin."

So, I did, and I noticed runners and cyclists turning their heads as they passed by the surgery. I could feel the edge of the knife cutting into my skin, and I closed my eyes but didn't make a sound. I didn't want to scare her and make her stop.

"Okay, I got it," she said. "You handled that well."

"Thanks. Unfortunately, this isn't the first time I have hooked myself today. And my embarrassment is subduing any pain I might feel," I responded. "I apologize; the humiliation has made me forget my manners. I am Michael," I added.

She reached out her hand, "I'm Aimee. It's very nice to meet you. So, how did this happen?"

I began to explain the whole thing, and when I said, "Well, you see, what had happened..." She stopped me.

"You know what, this is a story I want to hear in detail. I need to finish my run anyway. Want to meet up for drinks at the Fox and the Hound at around 7:30?" she asked.

"Sure, that sounds great," I replied, surprised I had somehow gotten a date out of this fiasco.

She turned and jogged off, I headed back across the river to my truck, so I could drive to my apartment. It was 5:30 p.m., and Sam was already gone. I had a text from him on my phone that said, "Call me." I mashed the call button on my phone as I left the parking lot.

"Hey, Sam. What's up?" I asked when I heard him answer.

"Hey, man. Did you catch anything by accident?" he asked.

"No, but I scored a date for tonight," I replied.

"What? How?" Sam asked.

"Long story. I am meeting her at the Fox later if you want to come up. I'll get a pool table, and we can hang out before going over to Woody's," I replied.

"Okay, sweet, is it okay if my sister tags along? She is in town visiting," Sam asked.

"Sure, that sounds even better. Having her there will balance things out a bit," I replied.

"What time?" he asked.

"The girl I met said 7:30 p.m., so about 6:45 or 7:00," I replied.

"Okay, see you there," Sam said and hung up.

I walked into my apartment as I dropped the phone from my ear then went to my bar to make a drink before getting in the shower. While I was in the shower, my cordless house phone sitting on my bathroom counter rang. I reached out, took a sip of my drink, then answered the phone.

"Hello," I said, standing in the tub but away from the water.

"Hey, man, can my sister and I come over to your place until it's time to go?" Sam asked.

"Yeah, man. The door is unlocked. I am in the shower now but still need to shave and stuff," I replied.

"Cool, see you in a few," Sam said.

I placed the phone back on the counter, took another sip, and finished my shower. I had half my face shaved when I heard my apartment door open.

"Hey, Mike, we're here, don't scare my sister," Sam yelled.

I heard ice dropping into some glasses in the kitchen.

"Hey, will you come to get my glass and pour me another? I got jeans on," I yelled from the bathroom.

Sam came to grab my glass and asked, "What's in it?"

"Vodka, water, and lime, thanks," I replied.

"So, Mike, tell me. How does a person meet a girl while standing in the middle of a damn river?" Sam asked as he walked over to my bar.

"Well, I wasn't standing in the middle of the river, for starters," I said loudly, so he could hear me.

"What? I thought you were trying to master the cast," he pressed.

"I was. It's a long, slightly embarrassing story," I responded, exiting the bathroom after putting on a white button-up shirt. "Hey, Jen," I said to Sam's sister.

"My favorite kind of story," Sam said as he handed me my drink.

"Yeah, I can't wait to hear this," Jen replied as she finished making her martini.

"It's a story I really only want to tell once, and I am going to have to tell it when I meet Aimee in a few anyway. Y'all can hear it then," I said.

"That means he is trying to figure out how to tell the story to make it less embarrassing," Sam said to his sister.

"Exactly," I smiled.

We finished our drinks, left, and arrived at Fox and the Hound at about 6:45, so we had time to get a pool table before Aimee got there. Much to my surprise, she was already sitting at the bar and saw us walk in.

"Hey there, this is Sam and his sister Jen. How was the rest of your run?" I said as we approached.

"Great! I laughed the whole way back," she said with a smile.

"Ouch, at least get a drink in me before throwing salt on the wound," I said with a chuckle.

"Oh, this is going to be really good," Sam laughed.

"Oh, you'll be alright. You know that shit's funny," she said; we both started laughing hysterically. "Speaking of wounds," she reached in her purse and pulled out a band-aid. "Turn around. I am sure you weren't able to get a bandage on the hole in your back."

"What the hell happened?" Jen laughed when she saw the cut in the middle of my back.

Sam instantly started laughing as hard as Aimee and me, saying, "The same thing that happened to his ear." Then he sat in the chair I had pulled out for me, next to Aimee. "Thanks, Mike; I needed a seat after seeing that."

"Come over here," Aimee gestured to her other side, away from Sam.

I turned around, and she dipped a napkin in her vodka, wiped the wound, put the bandage on the cut, and slapped the bandage after it was applied.

"There you go. Now tell me how this all happened. Then I'll tell them the part where I came in," she smiled and took a sip of her vodka.

"Well, you see, *I have spent all my memorable life fishing...*"

CHAPTER 6

FRIDAY NIGHT SMURF

By July of 2002, I had completed my first solo plumbing project, as mentioned in "A Building Blunder," but I hadn't learned yet how tragic that would turn out to be. So, at the moment, I was feeling pretty good about myself.

Tom, I, and every other available employee at Geep Mechanical had been working on a large food plant since October of 2001. Now in July, all five miles of the underground sewer had been installed. The concrete slab had been poured, and the main structure had been raised. I was now the lead apprentice, and Tom and I had developed a good working relationship. He still rode my ass, but messing with me wasn't as easy as it had been. However, every once in a while, Tom would pull out all the stops to show he could still get one over on me.

Once, while on the job in Duncanville, Tom pulled out his old, faded tool bag and acetylene torch. I thought it was strange because usually Tom just sat in his truck most of the day and read the newspaper while the rest of the plumbers worked. Tom reading the newspaper in his truck was fine with me for a couple of reasons. First, and most importantly, I always knew where he was. If he was in his truck, it meant he wasn't bothering me. Second, his responsibility was to make sure everything on the job was running smoothly. Tom had to ensure the other plumbers and I had all the necessary material to accomplish our designated tasks. It also required him to make on the spot decisions when the blueprints and real life didn't agree.

When I saw Tom pull his tool bag and torch out, I knew someone had missed something. Rather than have them go back and fix it, Tom would take it upon himself to correct the mistake. He claimed it saved time, but really it gave him a reason to mess with someone. Which, if you haven't been able to tell from other stories, was Tom's favorite pastime.

I was working on a second-floor mezzanine with a large open wall that looked over the parking lot. I was standing on a twelve-foot ladder installing a two-inch air line when I saw Tom go into one of the supply trailers Geep had on the site. He pulled a ten-foot piece of one-inch copper pipe and a handful of one-inch copper fittings from the trailer. I know it was still early because I made the mistake of asking Tom what he was working on when I headed out to morning break, which was always around 9:30 a.m.

"So, Tom, what has you scurrying around like a duck chasing a June bug?" I asked.

"None of your damn business, bitch!" Tom replied as we were all gathered around drinking coffee from the Roach Coach. Everyone laughed, including me.

"Easy there. Tom. You don't want to burn yourself out too early. You have a long day of trying to get under my skin," I responded.

"You sure talk a lot of crap for such a short stack of shit," Tom said.

"I am the same height as you, old man," I fired back.

"Yeah. I am sixty-eight-years-old. What's your excuse? When I was your age, I was six-foot. How tall are you?" Tom said.

"Five-foot-nine-inches," I answered proudly.

"Bullshit, you're not five-foot-nine!" Tom said. He then pulled out his tape measure and checked my height. "Okay, you are five-foot-nine, with those boots on. But without them, I bet you're five-seven."

"Five-eight, asshole! These aren't platforms!" I said emphatically.

"I have had enough of you already, Gump. Go back to work," Tom ordered.

"Gladly. The feeling is mutual, old man!" I responded.

Another plumber, Rick, and I were headed back into the building, "Boy, Tom is in a hell of a mood today," Rick said.

"Yeah, he gets pissed off anytime he has to get out in this heat and work," I said with a smile.

I went back to work installing the air line. When I had started the air line on Monday, I had a little more than 2,000 feet to assemble. Tom had bet me a lunch that I couldn't get done within the week. I accepted the bet and had no intent on losing. It was now Wednesday, and I had a little less than 1,000 feet left.

I climbed down the ladder at lunch and headed to my truck through the engine room and riser room. There in the riser room next to the large roll-up door was Tom. He was tapping a one-inch copper line into the four-inch water main. I was confused as to why because just the week prior, I had installed a four-inch backflow, a two-inch stub up for the roof, and continued the four-inch pipe into where the boiler room would be. I didn't see anything about a one-inch line on the prints when I was doing all of that. This meant Tom was fixing my mistake.

"Damn, Tom, did I miss a line?" I asked.

"Apparently, you did, Gump. Do you think I would be going through all of this if you hadn't?" Tom replied.

"No, sir. I am sorry. I can finish it after lunch if you prefer?" I offered.

"Why? So, you can screw it up even more? No, you just worry about that air line," Tom responded.

"Yes, sir," I replied, moderately defeated.

After having lunch with Len, Don, Rick, and a handful of other Geep employees, I went back to work running the air line as instructed. However, I felt ashamed knowing Tom was fixing something I had missed. At 2:30 p.m., I went out for an afternoon break. As I walked out of the large roll-up door, I saw Tom speaking with Len. As I approached, Tom saw me and walked off to his truck. I looked at Len and asked, "What was that all about?"

"Oh, Tom's just upset because he was bragging about you last week and now is fixing one of your mistakes," Len said. "Don't worry about it, though Gump, everyone makes mistakes." Len slapped me on the shoulder then went to Roach Coach for a Gatorade.

I went to my truck for some water I had in an ice chest. I pulled a towel from my cab and wiped the sweat from my face. Then I sat in the driver's seat, drank some water, and begged for the day to end without much else going wrong. When I saw Tom get out of his truck and head back into the riser room, I stepped out of my truck and headed in behind him. I walked in the large roll-up door, and immediately to the right was Tom working on the water line. Tom saw me and called out, "Get over here, Gump."

I scurried over and said, "Yes, sir?"

"Here, braze that piece of one-inch sticking out of that four-inch pipe, I might be pissed at you, but you're still the best at brazing copper on the job site," Tom said.

I grabbed Tom's torch and some brazing rods, then set to putting my very best weld on the copper. After I finished brazing the copper, I turned off the torch and set it down on Tom's bag. I looked over at him and said, "I really am sorry I missed this, Tom."

"Sorry doesn't fix it, does it, Gump? Go on, keep working on the air line. I can do the rest," Tom said in a calm disappointed tone.

I did as I was told and went back to installing the air line. I was now feeling even worse. The toughest part was Tom telling me I was the best at brazing and conveying disappointment with his tone. My stomach was in a knot.

At 5:00 p.m., the day was finally over. I gathered up my pair of twenty-four-inch, cast-iron pipe wrenches, my level, and a tape measure, then headed out to my truck. I walked through the riser room and saw Tom putting his tools in his bag. When I was about to the large roll-up door, Len called out from behind me, "Hey, Gump!"

I stopped dead in my tracks, turned around, and before I could mutter a word, WHAM! A one-inch jet of water hit me dead in the ear. My hardhat flew off and bounced across the concrete floor. I just stood there for about a second or two, getting drenched. My shoulders hunched over in defeat. Finally, I walked past the bent-over Tom and turned off the valve to the water line he had installed. I looked at Tom and said, "I didn't miss that water line, did I?"

"No," Tom said as he put his hand on my shoulder to keep from falling because he was laughing so hard.

Len, however, was already on his hands and knees, laughing hysterically.

"You really just spent all day putting in this water line just for this?" I asked, somewhat humiliated.

"Yep, and it was completely worth it. You were apologizing so much I had a hard time keeping a straight face. Especially when I got you to help by brazing that piece of one inch. I thought for sure you were going to look at the prints and figure out you hadn't missed anything," Tom laughed a little harder and tried to catch his breath, then continued. "Then the look on your face as your hardhat bounced across the ground. I am so glad you're here, Gump; it sure makes the week more fun," Tom finished, now laughing so hard that he was clenching his side.

"I am glad I am here for your amusement, Tom," I said as I, too, began to laugh.

"Not just his, Gump. That shit was great," Len said. "Now come help me up."

Knowing Len had terrible knees, I walked over and helped him up. As he and I walked back over to Tom, Tom said, "First thing tomorrow, take this apart and turn it into a hose station."

"You have got to be kidding me. You installed it to get me, and now I have to take it apart?" I asked.

"Yep, I won't be here tomorrow," Tom said.

"Yes, sir," I said reluctantly.

When Tom started that argument with me that morning at the break, he did so on purpose. He didn't care how tall I was; he just needed a reason to measure me so he could put the ninety-degree copper elbow in the right spot so the water would hit me in the ear. And when I walked out at afternoon break and saw Tom talking to Len, he told Len to get me to stop at the roll-up door. Tom had put an "x" with blue tape so Len would know when I needed to stop.

By late morning the following Friday, I had finished the air line and went out to Tom's truck to let him know.

"I got that air line done. Looks like you owe me lunch. Not today but next week sometime," I said to Tom through his open truck window.

"No one likes a show-off, Gump," Tom said with a smirk as he let out a stream of tobacco spit toward my feet.

"Yeah, especially those that lose a bet and owe the show-off a lunch," I laughed. "What should I do next?"

"I don't know. You're the big shot now. Go look at the prints and pick something," Tom barked.

"Yes, sir, and remember I am not working tomorrow," I said.

"Does Mike Callan have you working somewhere else?" Tom asked.

"No, sir, I have a date and have taken the weekend off. I have told you about it nearly every day this week," I replied.

"Yeah, I remember just surprised Mike hasn't ruined that for you yet," Tom said.

I left Tom's truck and headed back inside. But rather than head over to the plan table, I went over to where Len and Don were working.

"Hey Len, Don, how are y'all doing?" I asked.

"Not bad, Gump. What's up?" Len replied.

"Well, I have a date tonight and was wondering where I should take her for dinner?" I asked.

"Take her to Del Frisco's downtown. My daughter works there. I will tell her you're coming, and she'll hook you up," Len answered.

"Sweet. Thanks, Len," I said.

"You better get back to work, Gump. If Tom catches you over here jaw-jacking, he'll have your ass," Don chimed in.

"Yeah, I finished that air line and asked Tom what I should do next. He told me to pick something. It's so close to lunch I thought I would come bug y'all. I can find something after we eat," I said.

"What time is it, Gump?" Len asked.

I looked at my watch and said, "Eleven-fifteen."

"Well, you should make it appear as though you're looking over the prints. We have about thirty minutes here, and we'll swing by and get you on the way out," Len advised.

"Okay, I'll see you in a bit," I replied.

I then walked the 150 yards to the riser room. The plan table was just inside the large roll-up door where Tom's water line was. I stood over the blueprints looking for something that would keep me busy for at least a week. I wanted it to be challenging enough so I might coax Tom into another bet. Finally, Len and Don came through to get me.

"You ready, Gump?" Len asked.

"Yes, sir. Where are we going?" I asked.

"The barbecue joint," Len replied.

I nodded in agreement, took off my hardhat, and set it on the plan table. As we walked out toward the parking lot, I saw Tom reading the newspaper in his truck.

"Hey, guys, I am going to see if Tom wants to go and swing by my truck for my ball cap," I said and broke away from the group.

As I approached Tom's truck, he rolled down his window. "What do you want now, Gump?"

"I am just seeing if you want to go to the barbecue joint with us?" I asked.

"Nah, but thanks. I am going to walk through and see how far along everyone is, then just take a nap," Tom said.

"Okay, Tom. Don't work too hard," I said.

"Gump, I work harder getting out of bed than you do all day," Tom fired back.

I laughed, then I ran to my truck, grabbed my ball cap, and hurried over to Len's van. I opened the side door right behind the passenger door. These days I rode in the back tool cab. I had made myself a spot behind the driver's seat against the divider that separated the passenger cabin and the tool cab. There was a large square hole in the partition so Len could see into the back, which I used to communicate through. My seat was still an upside-down five-gallon bucket, and there wasn't any air-conditioning, but I had plenty of leg and elbow room, which was worth it.

After we got to the restaurant and were seated, Len asked, "So, Gump, who is this date?"

"A girl I met while fishing on the Trinity River," I responded.

"Wait, the girl who pulled the hook from your back?" Don asked.

"Yep, the very same. We have been trying to get together for weeks now, but I always end up canceling because of work." I replied.

"So, how many dates have you been on with this girl?" Len asked.

"This will be number three," I responded.

"Wow, three dates in three months. At this rate, you might get married by the time you're fifty," Len said. "Mikey, you better start telling Mike Callan, you can't work. Otherwise, you're going to look back one day and wonder where your life has gone," Len finished.

"Yeah, I know you're right, Len. It's just hard for me to say no when it comes to working," I replied with a sigh.

"How many hours did you work last week?" Len asked as he pulled a pen and a pad from his shirt pocket.

"Ninety-three," I replied quietly.

"And the week before that?" Len continued.

"Eighty-six," I said, almost ashamed.

"And the week before that?" Len pressed.

"Seventy-nine," I replied.

After some quick math, Len finished writing the numbers down and looked up at me, and said, "Mikey, that's an average of eighty-six hours a week. And, I know you have been working like this for at least the last eight months. That's nearly two years' worth of work in just eight months. I don't care how young you are; that ain't healthy."

"Yeah, again, I know you're right, Len," I said.

"Look, Mikey, I respect how hard you work. Hell, we all do, even Tom. That's why we pick on you so much. But why? Why do you damn near kill yourself every week?" Len asked sincerely.

"I don't know, Len. It's hard to explain," I replied.

"You don't know, or it's hard to explain? It can't be both," Don added.

"It's hard to explain, I guess," I responded, shrugging my shoulders.

"Okay, Gump. But you're going to slow down even if it means I start making work choices for you," Len finished.

"So, Gump, are y'all just going to dinner, or are you hoping for breakfast, too?" Don asked.

We all laughed and finished eating. Then we went back to work. I hopped out of the back of Len's van and saw Tom still taking a nap in his truck. I opened my truck door and tossed my ball cap back on the dashboard and walked into the job next to Don.

"Does it piss you off that all he does is sit in his truck and sleep or read the newspaper?" Don asked.

"Nope, because this way I always know where he is, and he isn't bothering me. Besides, as hot as it has been this summer, I'd be worried the old man would die of heatstroke. Not that I care if he dies, but everyone would think I killed him somehow," I said.

"Bullshit, Gump. You love that old goat, and you know it," Len chimed.

I just laughed and made my way back over to the plan table. I stood over the blueprints looking through them carefully for about ten minutes. Finally, I found exactly what I was looking for. A group of four two-inch copper water lines running together in a large loop around the food plant. They began in the boiler room and ran about five feet from the ceiling, about thirty feet in the air. Once I had all my pipe supports up, things would go really quickly. Basically, I could have about 2,500 feet of line in the air and done by next Friday. Which would make me look like a badass. The hardest part would be getting all the pipe supports made and hung. I looked at my watch and thought to myself, "It's 12:30 p.m. I have four-and-a-half hours left in the day. I should have enough time to get half of the 300 pipe supports assembled."

The pipe supports would be constructed of a galvanized steel Unistrut. I would have to cut the twenty-foot-long Unistrut into ten-foot lengths. The Unistrut would be the cross piece the pipe would rest in. The real trick was going to be the pieces of half-inch all-thread that would hang from the building's steel girders. Like all roofs, this one had a slope. For my pipe to be level, each pair of all-thread would have to be cut at different lengths. Luckily, I knew the roof's pitch, and with a bit of math, I was ready to get started. Once assembled, the pipe supports would look like a large metal trapeze.

I put on my hard hat and began gathering all the materials and tools I needed to start my pipe supports. I set up my workstation where the future loading dock would be. It was still hotter than the surface of the sun, but at least there was a little air moving through this portion of the building.

After I completed assembling my first five trapezes, I went ahead and hung them in the air and placed a ten-foot piece of pipe in them to make sure my math was correct and that the pipe would be level. Everything came out perfect, and I focused on getting the rest of the pipe supports completed by the end of the day.

At 2:30 p.m., it was time for the afternoon break. I was pleased I had gotten all my Unistrut cut, so I headed out to my truck, pulled a bottle of water from the ice chest in the bed then hopped into the cab. I pulled my phone from my glove box and began to text Aimee, "We are still on for tonight. See you @ 7."

Texting this simple message took nearly my entire fifteen-minute break because to type an "s" on my Nokia brick, you had to press seven a total of four times. If you missed the lowercase "s," you had to press seven nine more times to get back to it. Unfortunately, I couldn't call Aimee because she was taking summer classes at TCU to expedite her graduation.

After the break, I went back to the building and continued constructing my pipe hangers. I looked at my watch about 3:30 p.m. and found it strange Tom hadn't come by to see what I had chosen to work on next. I was rather upset about this because I really wanted to coax him into another bet. But, on days as hot as this, Tom rarely ventured out of his truck. I shrugged it off and went back to cutting all-thread.

About 4:30 p.m., I had assembled all but about fifty of the pipe supports. I felt pretty good about the day's progress and was confident I would have most the remaining supports done before leaving for the day. It was about this time that Len came by.

"Hey, Gump, Tom sent me over to make sure you aren't sleeping," Len said.

I looked up from my one-man-assembly-line to reply, but before I could, Len shouted, "Holy shit, Mikey, what's all over your face?"

"What do you mean?" I said, wiping my face. "Did I get it?"

"No, you better go look in a mirror somewhere," Len said as he began to chuckle. "I had nothing to do with this one, Mikey, I swear."

"Oh no! What now?" I said to Len as I made a beeline for my truck.

I got to the driver's door of my truck and folded the side-view mirror back. My jaw, heart, and stomach dropped when I saw the image looking back at me. Nearly my entire face was a streaked ocean blue. I took off my hardhat, and the blue began right where the sweatband of the hardhat sat. I instantly shot my enraged eyes over to Tom's truck and saw him peeking out from behind his newspaper. This was it; the old man had to die. I would have laughed it off any other day, but today I had a date. So, it was time I beat an old man's ass.

I dropped my hardhat and started toward Tom's truck with an angry stride. Tom folded up his newspaper, tossed it on his dashboard, put his truck in gear, and began to drive off. As he passed by me, Tom rolled down his window and said, "Just wear something blue, Gump. It looks good on you." I could still hear him laughing as he pulled out of the parking lot.

I walked back to my truck where I had dropped my hardhat. I picked it up, pulled down the sweatband, and instantly knew what Tom had done.

In construction, there is a tool called a chalk box or chalk line. A chalk box has a spool of string on the inside. One end of the spool is fed through an eyelet in the box. It also has a hook tied to the end of the string. The inside of the box can be filled with colored, powdered chalk. Chalk lines are used to pull between two points, and the string is popped to leave a straight line. You can buy chalk powder in many different colors, but Tom and I always used blue. Tom had filled the sweatband of my hardhat with the chalk box chalk.

Knowing Tom, I went over to my tool bag and opened it up. Laying there on top was my chalk-box. I opened the fill port and peered inside. Yep, it was empty. Not only did Tom fill my sweatband with chalk, but he also used all the chalk from my chalk box. I let out a yell of frustration. I wasn't sure I had ever been this angry.

I went back out to my truck, grabbed my towel from the cab, and dunked it in the melted ice of my ice chest. Then I went back to my truck door's mirror. I scrubbed my face praying the blue would come off. This, of course, was in vain. When the chalk mixed with my sweat, it turned into a dye. Because I had wiped my sweaty face with the dark brown jersey gloves I wore, I couldn't see the blue dye that was mixed with my sweat. I had been smearing my face for hours, effectively painting my face like a damn Easter egg.

I continued attempting to scrub the blue off with my towel but finally, I walked back into where Len and Don were working. They were picking up their tools for the end of the day when I approached. "Hey Len, is there any way to get this off?" I asked, my voice was mixed with desperation and anger.

Len and Don looked at me and began laughing uncontrollably. Then Len said, "I am sorry, Mikey. I know this isn't funny, but I can't help but laugh. Unfortunately, I have never seen that done, so I don't know anything."

"Have you called your date and told her yet?" Don asked, wiping tears from his eyes.

"No. She's still in class," I replied.

"Go ahead and head home, Mikey. We'll make sure everything gets picked up and locked away," Len said, also having to wipe tears from his eyes.

"Thanks," I replied.

I grabbed my tools and headed to my truck. When I pulled out of the parking lot, I sent Aimee a text, "Call me." It was 5:00 p.m., Aimee wouldn't get out of class until 6:00 p.m. I arrived at my apartment at 5:45 and as quickly as humanly possible, I got in the shower and began to scrub my face vigorously. First with a washrag, but that didn't work. So, I went to the kitchen and grabbed a new green scrub pad from under the sink. I got back in the shower and scrubbed until I felt I was removing the skin. I looked in the mirror, "Nope that didn't work either," I thought to myself. "Maybe if I shave." I lathered up my blue face and began to shave. I am not sure how but after shaving, the blue seemed darker. Suddenly, my phone rang. It was 6:00 p.m., and Aimee was calling. I answered the phone while looking in my bathroom mirror.

"Let me guess, you have to work tonight?" Aimee said angrily.

"No, I don't have to work tonight," I said.

"What do you have to work tomorrow and want to get to bed early?" Aimee pressed further.

"No, I don't have to work tomorrow. Something happened at work," I said.

Her tone changed to slightly concerned, and she asked, "Are you okay?"

"Yeah, I am, but I can't go out," I replied.

"What? Why?" Aimee asked, now back to half a yell.

"It's hard to explain. I just don't want to be seen in public," I replied.

"You had better damn well try to explain! We have been on two dates in three months. I understand that you work a lot, but this is becoming insane!" Aimee exclaimed.

"I understand, and you're right. I really wanted to go out with you tonight. I had reservations at Del Frisco's and took the whole weekend off," I said in defense.

"Then what the hell, Michael!" Aimee screamed through the phone.

"Look, I have stuff here. I can cook you dinner. I also have a fully stocked bar. If you're willing to stop by Blockbuster for a movie, we can still have a date. I just don't want to go out," I offered.

"Okay, fine. But I am getting a chick-flick, and you're going to like it," Aimee said, now somewhat calmed but forcing herself to yell as though she were still angry.

I gave Aimee my address, and she informed me she would be at my apartment at 8:00 p.m., sharp. She wanted a dry vodka martini waiting for her, and it had better still be cold. I agreed without argument. Honestly, I was more concerned about the current state of my face. When we hung up, I looked at my watch. I had just enough time to throw together a proper Italian meal. "This is where my time as a baker in high school pays off," I thought.

Aimee arrived promptly at 8:00 p.m. I had made angel hair pasta with homemade meat sauce. I also made a loaf of Italian bread from scratch. I was just starting to pour the martinis when Aimee knocked.

"Come in. It's open," I yelled. I heard the door open and let out a deep sigh, then turned to greet her.

When she saw my face, her jaw literally dropped open. For a few seconds, she just stood there speechless. Her eyes were wide and unblinking. Then she began laughing uncontrollably and fell to her hands and knees. She would look up at my face and begin laughing even harder. I am sure I was quite the spectacle. There I was in a pair of nice khaki slacks, a red button-up shirt, and a nice pair of boots. I was holding two freshly poured martinis and had a deep ocean blue face. After a few minutes of thinking about how I must look, I also began to laugh. I set the martinis on the coffee table and then sat on my couch. I had to offer a hand to Aimee so she could move from the floor to the sofa. We must have both laughed for several minutes because it was the timer on the oven, telling me to pull the bread, that finally interrupted the laughter.

After pulling the bread, I returned to the couch, sat next to Aimee, and took a sip of my martini.

"Wow, I think this might be better than the first time we met," Aimee said as she took a tissue from her purse to wipe the tears.

"I don't know. You pulling a hook from my back is a pretty funny first meeting," I responded.

"Well, at this rate, I can stop doing ab work in the gym. Dating you certainly isn't dull, Michael," Aimee said. She went to take a sip of her drink, then spit half of it out because she looked at my face and started laughing again.

"Well, I am glad I can be entertaining, at least," I said.

"Yeah, we just have to work on your availability," Aimee said.

"You're the second person to say something like that today," I responded.

"Before we go any further, I have to say the food smells amazing. I was expecting hamburgers or hotdogs, not an entire Italian meal. We can eat when we watch the movie. First, tell me how this happened," Aimee said.

So, I told her what had happened to receive a blue face. I also filled her in on the incident earlier in the week. After the stories were told, Aimee asked, "So, does this sort of thing happen a lot?"

"Does this happen a lot," I said, pointing to my face. "No, this is a first. And I'll be plotting my revenge, I can assure you. But yeah, I get a lot of pranks played on me."

"Then why do you still work there?" Aimee asked.

"At this point, I am really not sure. But at least it's never dull," I replied laughingly.

"Well, let's eat and watch the movie," Aimee said.

"What did you get?" I asked.

"All the Pretty Horses," Aimee answered.

"Awesome, I have been wanting to see that movie," I said sarcastically.

"You'll live. Afterward, we can have one more drink before we go to bed," Aimee smiled.

"Oh really? Before WE go to bed?" I said curiously.

"Oh yeah. It's not every night a girl gets to sleep with a smurf."

CHAPTER 7

A TWENTY-DOLLAR LESSON

W hen I was twenty-three, things in my life really began to take shape. I was doing really well at Geep Mechanical and had gained the respect of all the employees, even Tom. I had received several raises and was making really good money for a twenty-three-year-old. I still worked too much to sustain any meaningful relationship, though.

Aimee and I broke up in the fall of 2003. She had finished her bachelor's degree at Texas Christian University and transferred to Florida State to pursue her master's in marine biology. We talked about having me move there with her, and I seriously considered making the leap. Unfortunately, at the time, making a jump like that was a bit too daunting for me. We didn't kid ourselves about maintaining a long-distance relationship. We enjoyed the rest of our time together, and I helped her pack up her apartment into a U-Haul. When I closed the back of the truck and walked her to the driver's side door, I said, "Call when you stop for the night."

"Of course. Don't work too much. And try not to get any more hooks stuck in your back," Aimee said, trying to force a smile.

I took off my cowboy hat. We exchanged "I love you's," and "I'll never forget you's," and one more long goodbye kiss. Then she climbed behind the wheel; I closed the door and watched her drive away. After Aimee called to let me know she had made it a couple of days later, I never heard from her again.

Many good things came out of my relationship with Aimee. Most importantly, I had learned to tell Mike Callan no more frequently so I could spend more time with her. I still worked sixty to seventy hours a week, which proved more acceptable to Aimee.

Len, of course, really helped after Aimee's departure. Every time I saw him, he asked, "You're still here?"

"Yes?" I would respond curiously.

"I just thought you would've quit by now and moved to Florida," Len would say half-jokingly.

"Nah, not yet," I'd laugh.

"Probably a good thing. Too many hurricanes anyway. Knowing you, you'd have tried to ride an alligator and been eaten," Len would laugh.

At least once a month, Len would take control of my work decisions and tell Mike Callan, "Mikey can't work this weekend. He is going with me to a Texas music concert."

Most of the time, it was just a show at Woody's Tavern. Every Thursday through Saturday, Woody's Tavern had live Texas music. I had learned not to argue with Len. One time I disobeyed his intervention, and the next few weeks were filled with Len harassing me with practical jokes or messing with my head. I genuinely enjoyed hanging out with Len and his gang for the weekend anyway because, surprisingly, Len turned out to be a fantastic wingman. He would introduce me to a girl he knew somehow. Usually, friends of his daughters or just someone Len had started talking to so he could introduce me. He really enjoyed introducing me because almost every introduction came at the cost of my ego. But I had grown used to it and now just laughed along because it really helped break the ice.

One Friday night, I was sitting at my apartment, getting ready to have an early dinner and head to bed. I had to be at work early the next morning at a food plant. The facility would be shut down so that Geep Mechanical could replace a boiler. I knew I was in for a long and hard weekend, so, like an athlete preparing for a marathon, I had made a large pot of pasta with some steak. As I sat down to watch a little TV and eat, my cellphone rang suddenly. It was Mike Callan.

"Well, Mikey, I hate to completely ruin your weekend, but tomorrow's shut down has been canceled. You can come into the shop and inventory pipe fittings if you absolutely want to work," he said.

"Well, damn it," I laughed. "As great as that sounds, I think I'll force myself to enjoy the workless weekend."

"Okay, Mikey. If you're sure, you can handle all the free time. Have a nice weekend," Mike said.

"Thank you, sir; you, too," I responded and ended the call. I instantly called my buddy Sam.

"What's up, Mike?" Sam answered.

"Hey, man. I just got the weekend off. Do you want to do something?" I asked.

"Sure. What'd you have in mind? Woody's?" Sam asked.

"No. How about for once we do something different? I am going to eat real quick and get dressed. I can pick you up in about an hour," I said.

"What did you make? I haven't eaten yet, and now don't want to take the time to cook something," Sam said.

"Steak and pasta. I can save half of this steak for you, and there is plenty of pasta," I responded.

"Damn, sounds great. Am I dressing for downtown or the Stockyards?" Sam asked.

"Somewhere in the middle. I think I can find a concert or something," I said.

"Cool, I'll text you when I am on my way," Sam said and hung up.

I looked at my phone, and it was only 4:30 p.m. I cut my steak in half and threw it in the oven to stay warm. Then I watched some more TV. I had already showered, so getting ready wouldn't take long. I got a text from Sam about thirty minutes later that he was en route. He only lived about five minutes away, so I started getting myself ready for a night out. I was in the bathroom when I heard my apartment door open.

"Don't shoot; I am just robbing your bar and food," Sam called out.

"Cool, steak is in the oven. Make me a whiskey on the rocks. Will ya?" I responded.

"Yep, I'm on it. So, what exactly are we doing?" Sam asked.

"Well, I heard Len say something about Cross Canadian Ragweed playing somewhere. He hasn't answered his phone, so I checked the newspaper. Looks like we are headed to Lonestar Park," I said.

"Awesome. Sounds like a target-rich environment. Can I borrow some cologne?" Sam replied.

I walked out of my bathroom and retrieved my drink from Sam. "Sure, do you want to use my toothpaste and deodorant, too?" I laughed.

After we finished our drinks and Sam finished eating, we headed out the door. On our way out to Lonestar, Sam told me about his week in the electrical world, and I filled him in on the latest happenings at Geep.

Lonestar Park is a horse racing track located in Grand Prairie, Texas. During this era, they often had concerts on weekends after the final set of races. When we arrived at Lonestar, we bought our tickets and walked into the Downs. We hit the beer stands and could tell with our first purchases it would be an expensive night. But we didn't party like this often, so what the hell.

After getting our beers, we saw where the stage was and decided to watch the last few races before the concert began. While we were walking around trying to find a place to sit, I heard a familiar voice call out, "Hey, Gump!"

I instinctively ducked and looked around. I then saw Len stand up and wave his hand in a gesture to join him and his usual group of friends.

"What the hell are you doing here? I thought you had to work tomorrow?" Len asked.

"I told Mike Callan to shove it up to his ass. I wanted to come to Cross Canadian Ragweed," I said.

Len laughed and replied, "Bullshit. I wish you would do that. But bullshit."

"Nah, Mike Callan called me and said they canceled the shutdown tomorrow. I remembered you saying something about this, so Sam and I decided we would break away from the norm," I replied.

"Well, awesome. Y'all have a seat. It's going to be a long night of standing, so y'all better rest those legs while you can," Len said as he shook Sam's hand.

Len and Sam knew each other not only through me, but Sam worked for Len's brother, Lee.

About fifteen minutes before the last race was over, we got up from our table to get drinks and secure our standing area near the stage.

At this time in Cross Canadian Ragweed's career, their most popular song was "The Boys from Oklahoma Roll their Joints all Wrong." They must have been playing it a lot because when they finally came out on stage, they said, "Don't ask us to play Boys from Oklahoma. It's not on our playlist, and we aren't going to do it." Like any respectable crowd of Texans, we all started chanting "Boys from Oklahoma." Cross Canadian Ragweed opened with a song called "Carney Man" but naturally caved into peer pressure and played "Boys from Oklahoma" next.

Toward the end of the first set, a genuinely odd thing happened. People down around the front of the stage were dancing, and suddenly a mosh pit erupted. I wasn't a virgin to mosh pits, but this was the first I had seen at a Texas music event. But, because I hate being left out of a unique experience, I decided to jump in. My cowboy hat was knocked off, and I took an elbow to the eye, but I was grinning from ear to ear. Then, out of nowhere, I felt myself being lifted to the heavens and could feel God's grip on my shoulder pulling me skyward. It wasn't God, though; it was Len. His vice-like grip was pulling me from the crowd. I went to jump back into the pit, but Len put his hand on me and said, "Hold on there, wild man." A second later, a swarm of police officers came in and broke up the mayhem not so politely. My eye was a little bruised, my lip was busted and bleeding, but I wasn't being tossed from the concert or worse, thanks to Len.

Len pulled out his wallet, handed me a twenty, and said, "How about you go get me a beer and cool off before the lines get longer than they already are."

I agreed, took his twenty, then went to grab my cowboy hat from a kind stranger who had rescued it from being trampled. I fixed a few dents it had taken, placed it back on my head, and began the uphill trek to the concessions. I went to the Crown Royal line first to get myself something to sip on while waiting in the beer line. I paid for the high-priced whiskey with my money, then went to the long beer line. Unfortunately, by the time I got to the front, I was out of Crown and my own cash. So, I decided to get myself a Budweiser and Len a Bud Light, with his twenty. Beers were eight dollars each, and after I gave the girl a tip, I only had a dollar left to hand Len as change. I wasn't too worried, though; there was an ATM inside, so I would just get the next round.

As I walked back to Len, a girl stopped me and asked, "How do you know Len?"

"We work together. How do you know him?" I asked in return.

"I am friends with his daughters," she replied.

She and I talked for a bit longer than I had intended. When we finished, I looked down at the beers, and not only had I drank all of mine but half of Len's, too. "I am going to catch hell for this," I thought to myself and made my way down to our standing area. I walked up to Len, handed him the half-full cup of beer, and waited for the expected response.

Len looked at the cup, then at me, and said, "What's this?"

"Your beer," I said with a smile.

"Where's the rest of it?" Len pressed. I could tell he was half-pissed and half-amused.

"I drank it. Those lines were long," I replied.

"What the hell, Gump? Where's my change?" Len asked. He was now laughing and looked at his friend Danny Page and said, "Do you believe this guy?"

I reached in my pocket and pulled out the dollar along with about seventy-five cents in an assortment of coins I had brought from home. I handed it to Len and waited.

"What the hell is this?" Len asked, now laughing even harder.

"Your change," I snorted.

"What? Where's the rest?" Len shouted as he continued to laugh.

"Well, I had to get myself a beer, also. You know, as a service charge. Then the poor girl pouring beers deserved a tip. After that, you had a dollar left. The coins are actually mine."

Len stood there trying to fathom the stunt I had just pulled, his hand still outstretched with the change.

"In fact, let me get that quarter. Sam and I will probably play some pool at the Oui after this," I said, reaching for the quarter.

"Get the hell out of here." Len laughed, closing his hand and swatting mine away. "Where the hell is your beer?"

"Oh, I drank that, too, when I stopped to talk to a girl. Thanks for that, too, by the way. She actually stopped me to ask how I knew you," I said.

"Well, I hope it was a good conversation?" Len said.

"It was, I think I might get a date out of it, thanks," I replied, as I slapped Len on the shoulder while regaining my composure.

Len took a drink of the beer then dumped the rest of it out, "It's gotten hot."

"Of course it has. I was talking to her for at least an hour," I laughed. "Don't fret, Len. I am going to go up and get us a couple of more."

"No. Don't do me any favors. I'll go get my own. You just give me twenty after you hit the ATM," Len said.

"Are you sure? I am going up there anyway," I asked.

"Yeah, I am sure your little pea brain would probably see a squirrel and get lost," Len replied.

I shrugged my shoulders and walked back up to the pavilion. I realized through all of this I hadn't seen, Sam. I pulled out my phone to call him, but he didn't answer. I went to the ATM and withdrew another one hundred dollars, then went to get another beer. Len was right not to have me get him a refill because I began talking to another girl while standing in line. Once again, the conversation went on far longer than intended.

When I got back to Len, he asked, "Did you get lost?"

"Nah, just got sidetracked. Here's that twenty," I said, holding out a fresh twenty-dollar bill.

"No, you keep it. You can pay me back on Monday. Who knows how many more times you'll get sidetracked," Len smiled.

I put the twenty back in my pocket and didn't think any more of it. By the end of the concert, I still hadn't seen Sam, so I tried calling him again. Finally, he answered.

"What's up, man?" Sam said when he answered.

"Hey, where are you?" I asked.

"I met someone, and we decided to leave a little early," Sam responded.

"Oh, okay, cool. I'll talk to you later then. Call me if you need a ride tomorrow," I replied and ended the call. I made my way to my truck and decided to call it a night, so I headed home.

The following Monday, I saw Len at work and went over to pay him the twenty dollars. "Hey, Len, here's that twenty," I said, trying to hand him the cash.

"Nah, Mikey, you keep it and pay me on Friday after we get paid," Len said.

"Thanks, but no need, Len, I am flush," I replied, still trying to hand him the twenty.

"Okay, still, just keep it. You can buy the first round of drinks this weekend," Len said.

"Okay, that sounds fair," I replied. I knew Len was planning something at my expense, but I had no idea what it could be. Whatever it was, I knew trying to repay him was now pointless.

The following weekend, Len and I were at Woody's Tavern. I went to buy Len's first round, but he refused. "Nah, Mikey, you can buy the shots when we start doing them. They're more expensive anyway," he said.

"I have never worked so hard trying to pay someone back before. What is he up to?" I thought to myself. It wouldn't be long before I found out.

The band playing this particular weekend was called Thrift Store Cowboys, and a nice crowd was starting to arrive at Woody's. Len's usual group of friends were in attendance at their regular set of tables near the small dance floor in front of the stage. Sam and I had our own group we hung out with around the pool tables. I could typically hustle up enough money in games to cover my tab at the end of the night. While I was waiting for Sam to show, I sat with Len and company, listening to the conversations while drinking my usual Bacardi and Coke with a lime. My glass was nearly empty, so I stood to go get another. It was then that Danny Page held out a ten-dollar bill and said, "Get me one, too, will you, Mikey?"

I reached for the ten when Len grabbed it first and handed it back to Danny. "I wouldn't do that, Danny," Len began. "You'll never see your drink or your ten-dollars again. Gump still owes me twenty from last weekend," Len finished.

"No? That can't be true. Mikey is more responsible than that, I'm sure," Danny replied, clearly setting up Len's attack. I just sat back down in my chair because I knew what was coming. Len not letting me pay him back was all part of whatever was about to happen next.

"Last weekend while at Cross Canadian Ragweed," Len said

loudly, getting everyone's attention, "I gave Gump a twenty and asked him to get me a beer. I would have made the trip myself, but y'all know how my knees start to hurt after standing too long."

"Great, he is gaining sympathy. This is going to be bad," I thought. I could feel myself turning red already.

"Gump, took my money and said, no problem, and assured me he would be back as soon as he could. But you didn't come back as soon as you could, did you, Gump?" Len was looking at me, begging me to respond. His face was sad, but his eyes were glistening. I could see the demon inside him laughing.

"No, Len, I didn't," I said calmly, letting out a little chuckle because I knew my fate was sealed.

"No, you didn't. And, for an hour, you left me dying of thirst," Len added in a convincing, traumatized tone.

"Okay, I think you're laying it on a little thick," I said. I instantly knew I had broken a critical rule of survival. When you find yourself as one of Len's targets, never offer ammunition by speaking.

"Oh, really, Gump? I am laying it on thick. You don't think I was thirsty after saving you from certain death?"

"Whatever do you mean, Len?" Danny chimed, right on cue.

"Of course, you're in on this," I said with my face, shooting a glare at Danny. He just slightly smiled.

Then Len continued, "Mikey was in that stupid rumble pit that broke out during the first set. I saw the cops coming to start busting heads and reached in and pulled him out."

"No. Is that true, Mikey?" Danny asked with a subtle hint of sarcasm.

"Yes, it's true, but..." I began, but Len interrupted.

"But, what, Mikey?" Len asked.

"Nothing. Yes, it's true," I leaned back, awaiting the final blow.

"What's worse," Len said, now talking to the entire group, "is not only did Mikey not return with my beer after being gone for over an hour, but he brought me half a beer and only one dollar in change."

"What? How did that happen?" Danny asked Len.

"I don't know. How did that happen, Mikey?" Len asked. His face somehow looked disappointed, but I could see him smile as he lifted his glass of Crown to his lips.

"Len's not going to deliver the kill shot. He has loaded the weapon and is now forcing me to pull the trigger," I thought to myself. "I had bought myself a beer, too," I said aloud.

"And why had you returned with only half a beer when you had bought two, with my money?" Len pressed.

"Because I had drunk them both," I replied.

Everyone's mouths dropped open in shock. My character had successfully been tarnished. But Len wasn't done.

"And what was so important that it took you an hour to get back to me but had time to drink two beers?" Len asked.

This was it, the nail in the coffin, and I was going to nail it shut from the inside. "I stopped to talk to a girl," I said and dropped my head onto the table. "But I tried to pay you back that night, but you refused. I have also been trying to pay you back all week," I cried out in defense.

"Really, Mikey, do you think anyone here believes that if you had tried to pay me back, I wouldn't accept it," Len said. I could see his demon soul doing cartwheels, but his face only showed pure disappointment.

"Ah, hell, I'm done," I said. I got up and walked to the bar.

Len and Danny came up to the bar a few moments later. Danny stood to my left and Len to my right. Len put his hand on my shoulder and said, "Thanks Gump, that was fun."

"Yeah, the look on your face when you realized why Len hadn't let you pay him back was great to witness," Danny added.

"It's your world, Len, and sometimes it's hell having to live in it," I laughed. "When did you guys come up with this?"

"That very night when you left to go back up to the Pavilion," Len replied.

I wasn't upset; I was impressed. I had just learned a new tactic for messing with someone. Len and Danny returned to their group, and I naturally stayed up at the bar. I had finished about two drinks when Sam finally showed up, and we went over to begin playing pool. I told Sam about the events that had just occurred, and Sam was upset he had missed the transaction. About an hour into our pool games, Len sent me a shot of Crown Royal. When I looked over at him, he raised his glass, toasting to his victory from across the room.

Len never let me pay back those twenty dollars just so he could bring it up every few months for a well-timed dig. He always told me, after the abuse was done, "Gump, that was the best twenty dollars I have ever given someone."

CHAPTER 8

DAVID VS. GOLIATH

A few months after the epic night with Len, mentioned in "A Twenty Dollar Lesson," I was in another local establishment called The Mule. Len was going to meet me there because it was a favorite spot when he was in his twenties and wanted to see how much had changed. But The Mule operated under another name in Len's youth.

I liked The Mule because it was another place I often went to hustle a few games of pool. On a good night, I could generally walk out with a couple of hundred dollars. So, I tried to make sure to visit the place once a month.

Len arrived about half an hour after I did. I was still sitting up at the bar, waiting for a decent crowd to show. I was hoping a rich TCU student would show up with some of his friends and girlfriends. I could generally play on their egos and talk them into a high-dollar game, so they didn't look like cowards in front of their group. When Len arrived, he came up to the bar and ordered a drink. After only five minutes, he saw someone he knew. It was pretty typical for Len to see someone he knew just about anywhere he went in Fort Worth. Far too often when we would be out to lunch he would have to stop and talk to someone he hadn't seen in a while. It happened so often, in fact, I called him Mr. Mayor after an encounter. When Len moved down the bar to talk to his old acquaintance, I spotted a good target at the pool tables, so I decided to make my move.

I had found my group of TCU students I had been hoping for: three college guys with their girlfriends. I convinced them to play teams, and I partnered with their third. We started out playing for drinks, and either the kid on my team was utterly ignorant of the game of pool, or he was purposely trying to lose. After a couple of games, I had lost one and won one. It was now time to see if they were willing to gamble their parents' money. I didn't want to scare them off, so I started with my standard line. "We are playing faster than I can drink. How about we play for five dollars a stick?" I waited for a response as the three of them talked it over. I was certain they were strategizing my demise. I wasn't terribly concerned, though, because I was a pretty good pool player at this time in my life, and only one of them posed a real threat as far as talent was concerned.

After a few minutes, they came back and agreed so long as we kept the same teams. I was happy to fold to their terms. I went up to the bar and had the bartender make me water with lime in such a manner that it looked like I was drinking vodka and water. Then I went to work winning enough games to stay ahead but losing one every now and then to make them feel like they still had a chance. After a couple of hours, I had my opponents down one hundred dollars and had convinced them to play one last game for double or nothing. I was staring two hundred dollars in the eye. My only concern was my partner. I had to do my best to have an incredible break so that maybe I could run the table afterward, effectively taking my partner out of the equation.

My opponents racked the pool balls in the standard eight-ball formation. I walked around the table, chalking my pool cue and making sure the pool balls were racked tightly. Everything had to be perfect if I had any chance of pulling this off. I placed the cue ball at the other end of the table but not dead center like I had been all night. No, this break would require a unique alignment.

The rails of a pool table have dots that run along their tops. I set the cue-ball one dot to the right on the back rail and one dot forward on the right rail. Then I put down my pool stick and went to the pool cue rack and grabbed the heaviest cue I could find. I would only use this pool stick to break with, then switch to the lighter one I had used all night to finish the game. I asked the waitress that had come on shift to bring me a Bacardi and coke, then lit up a cigarette. Depending on how this break went, I might need them both to settle my nerves.

I lined up behind the cue ball and settled into my stance. I squatted with my knees and bent my upper body forward at the waist until the pool cue was parallel with the playing surface. I put all my weight on my back foot so I could step through the stroke with as much force as possible. I was set. I took a deep breath and let loose a break like the cue ball was a bullet, and I was the rifle.

The cue ball made contact with the first and second ball of the rack at the exact same time. The triangle formation of balls erupted in an explosion turning the pool table into a field of chaos. The sound of the eruption was so loud that the bar fell silent for a moment, and I could feel all eyes looking in my direction. Through the chaos, my eyes were drawn to one ball that had begun to move with substantial speed; it was the eight ball. It hit the back rail hard, then moved to the left-side rail. After the eight ball hit the side rail, it tracked toward the right-side pocket, but it was slowing considerably. "Does it have enough?" I thought to myself. I held my breath and stood there silently watching. Time seemed to drag on forever as I waited. Slowly, the eight ball came to the edge of the pocket and seemed to stop for a second, then teetered into the pocket.

I had taken Judas out of the picture with one shot and won two hundred dollars. I politely shook my opponents' hands and accepted my reward. There was no reason to gloat, it was mostly luck that had won me the game, and I was fully aware. It wasn't the first time I had made the eight ball on the break, but it was the first time I had done it when it really counted. I grabbed my cigarette, and the waitress brought my drink. She had been watching the event unfold because she knew the stakes were high. She planted a great big kiss on me and said, "That was the most exciting break I have ever seen. It was like I was watching a movie."

"Well, it's more exciting now, and you played your part in the movie perfectly," I said with a smile. I had been looking for a chance to ask her out for a few weeks and finally had the opportunity. "Want to grab something to eat at Ol' South Pancake House when you get off work tonight?"

"Sure, I would love to," she responded.

"Great, I'll be back up here at 2:30 a.m. Or do you just want to meet there?" I asked.

"Meet here, and we can ride there together," she responded.

"Awesome, it's a date," I said.

I headed back down the length of the bar. Not only had I just won two hundred dollars, but I had also scored a date. It was turning out to be quite a night, and it was only 10:30 p.m. I got back to where Len was and told him the incredible news.

"Len, I just won two hundred bucks and got myself a date at Ol' South with the waitress," I said.

Len looked at his friends and said, "This asshole still owes me twenty dollars and is bragging about winning two hundred."

I pulled a twenty from my pocket and said, "Here, take it, please. I am tired of hearing about it."

"No, Mikey, you'll probably need it for your big date," Len said.

"I am going to go down to the other end and talk to someone I don't owe money to. Let me know when you're ready to head to Woody's," I said.

I was walking my way down the bar, stopping to talk to a few of the regulars I knew along the way. My plan was to go set up next to where the waitress pulled drinks from the bar and chat with her while I could. On my way to the spot I was heading to, I bumped into a person who had their rear end sticking halfway into the walkway. I politely said excuse me and continued along my way. I arrived at my spot next to the bar and started a conversation with a patron sitting there. He was also a regular I knew. He and I had played in a pool league together and often swapped stories about hustles. His pool shark days were pretty much over, but he didn't mind telling some old tricks he had pulled. He and I talked for about half an hour until I saw Len hold up his drink, letting me know it would be his last. I asked the bartender to deliver me another drink next to Len at the other end of the bar. I then said my goodbyes to the waitress and my fellow pool player. As I made my way back toward Len, my waitress called out, "Don't forget about me?"

I turned and smiled, then said, "Don't worry darling, I have waited too long to get a chance with you."

As I was turned toward the waitress, I continued to walk backward, then I bumped into the same guy I had before. His lower end was stuck out, still blocking half the walkway. Still, feeling a little cocky from my victory and primed with a little more alcohol, I decided to say something this time. "Hey there, Doublewide, how about parking that trailer a little closer to the curb."

Then rose a man who took half a century to stand up straight. He must have been about six-foot-six because I was staring at the center of his chest when he finished growing. Doublewide was a great nickname because his shoulders were so broad I doubt they would fit through a set of double doors. The Dallas Cowboys had missed half their offensive line by not drafting this guy. I guess he was bent over the way he was so that he would be down low enough to talk to all of us little people.

"Excuse me?" Doublewide said, obviously not amused with my sense of humor.

"Think quick, Mikey. Your life depends on it," I thought. "That's all right; you're excused," I said as I slapped his shoulder, trying to walk past him. Unfortunately, the double doors didn't open.

"I am sorry. Do you care to rephrase that?" Doublewide said, putting his hand on my chest.

"Not particularly. Do you have trouble understanding the English language?" I responded, removing his hand from my chest. "This is going to hurt," I thought to myself as the words flew from my mouth. Somehow, I had lost the ability to keep my damn mouth shut.

"You talk a lot of shit for a little guy who's about to get his ass kicked," Doublewide said. At this point, I couldn't really disagree.

"Yeah, well, dynamite comes in small packages, dipshit," I fired back.

Then Doublewide did something that perfectly displayed just how outmatched I truly was. He reached down, placing one giant hand on my left arm and his other massive paw on my right arm, pinning them to my side. Then he lifted me off the ground, brought me up to his eye level, and said softly, "Explode then, bitch."

My eyes were wide, my mind went blank, and I couldn't think of anything to say.

"What's the matter, small fry? Is something wrong?" Doublewide said with a smile.

"Dale, is that you?" I heard a familiar voice say. It was Len. "It is you. How are you doing?" Len asked Doublewide.

"Hey, Len, what are you doing here?" Dale the Doublewide responded, still holding me in the air.

"Oh, just checking out the old stomping grounds," Len said. "Hey, Gump, what are you doing hanging around here?" Len asked as he looked at me.

"You know this little shit?" Dale asked Len, finally putting me down.

"Yeah, he works with me. He's a hell of a worker but not too bright. That's why we call him Gump," Len returned.

"Well, Gump needs to learn some manners," Dale said.

"Oh, he has plenty of manners. He just gets a little cocky, sometimes, and forgets how to use them," Len said to Dale. "You have manners, don't you, Gump," Len said as he looked at me. His voice was in the tone of a coach that had just gotten you a second chance on a final, so you can still play ball.

"Yes, sir," I said to Len.

"My apologies, sir. Can I buy you a beer?" I said to Dale, knowing I had bitten off more than I could chew.

"No, but you can buy all three of us shots, with that two hundred dollars you have been bragging about for an hour," Dale replied.

"Yes, sir, I'd be happy to," I responded.

So, I bought all of us shots of Crown Royal. Turns out Dale and Len had worked together on a couple of jobs back when Len was younger. Dale and Len told a few stories from when The Mule was known as The Pig and the Whistle. Dale commented that he liked my courage to follow through even if I was looking at utter destruction. We finished our conversation then Len and I then went down to the other end of the bar to have another drink before heading to Woody's.

"That's twice in three months I have had to save your life, Gump. Maybe I should collect that twenty dollars after all. At this rate, you aren't going to live long enough for me to get much more fun out of it." Len chuckled.

"Yeah, I really didn't see that going that way," I responded.

"What did you say that made him pick you up?" Len asked.

"He called me small, so I told him dynamite comes in small packages. Then he picked me up and told me to explode," I replied as I started to laugh hysterically. Len spit his drink out all over the bar and also began to laugh.

"Yeah, that's a pretty good response. What were you going to do if I hadn't stepped in?" Len asked.

"I am not sure. I was working on that. My plan was dependent on him hitting me, not picking me up," I responded.

"Oh yeah? What was that plan like then?" Len pressed, looking at me with genuine curiosity.

"Hopefully, ducking, kicking him in the knee, and running for the door. After he picked me up, the only thing I could think of was how expensive the cab ride home from the hospital was going to be," I said. Then Len and I both started laughing again.

"Well, did you learn anything, Mikey?" Len asked.

"Yeah, I sure did," I responded.

"Good, what did you learn? I want to make sure it's the right lesson," Len said.

"That if you're going to pick a fight with Goliath, you had better have planned as well as David and made damn sure God is on your side," I laughed.

Needless to say, Len enjoyed making me tell this story whenever he could work it into an evening. Generally, right after he told anyone that would listen about me owing him twenty dollars.

Chapter 9

The Vacations of 2004

Part One: Cozumel

During my entire tenure at Geep Mechanical, I don't remember ever having a holiday off. I even worked Thanksgiving and Christmas, mainly because my family celebrated those holidays on their Eves. It was, of course, my fault for always working holidays because I never said, "No, I don't want to work this holiday." However, the habit of working holidays would come to a head in 2003 when the family had gathered at one of my sisters' houses for Christmas Eve.

A particular food plant had become known as "My Baby" because nearly every night between midnight and 4:00 a.m., I was at the plant fixing something. Obviously, baby was an accurate nickname for the plant because it required constant attention, attention I gave nearly every night and at least one full day most weekends. My usual work week in 2003 consisted of waking up on Monday and going to Geep's construction site until 5:00 p.m., then on to "My Baby" to speak with the maintenance supervisor. He would give me a list of anything that had popped up on Sunday or over the weekend if I were tasked somewhere else.

I would assure the supervisor I would fix whatever leaks on the list I could during the sanitation shutdowns between midnight and 4:00 a.m. If there were any other leaks I saw, I would do my best to fix those as well. If I couldn't get them all, I would add whatever was left to my weekend list. I would work on the construction site from 7:00 a.m. until 4:00 p.m. for the rest of the week. I would leave the construction site early enough to swing by a plumbing supply store to gather materials for the set of leaks I would fix that particular night. Then I would go home to get some rest. I would head to "My Baby" at 10:30 p.m. so I could be ready to start shutting things off right at midnight. When the plant fired back up at 4:00 a.m., I would drive straight to the construction site and sleep in my truck until 6:50 a.m. Then start the whole process over again. "My Baby" had over twenty miles of copper water lines, nearly ten miles of steam lines, and several miles of a myriad of other types of piping. There was always something to fix.

I remember it was cold on Christmas Eve in 2003 because my sister had me pull the large, tree-like propane heater into the garage and set up a table with plenty of chairs for every member the family. This was so the family could sit in the garage to drink and smoke comfortably. After dinner was had and presents had been opened, nearly the entire family was in the garage smoking cigarettes and sipping their favorite beverages. I must have been paying too much attention to my watch because my father noticed and asked, "What's the matter, Michael? Do you have medication to take?"

"No, sir. I just need to leave at ten o'clock," I responded.

"What? Why?" my brother chimed immediately.

"I have to work," I replied.

"Who works on Christmas Eve?" my brother pressed further, slightly perturbed.

"Apparently, I do. My world doesn't stop because of a holiday. If anything, that's when I need to work the most," I said.

"Don't you think the amount you're working is getting a little out of hand?" my brother asked sincerely.

"Perhaps, but I have already committed to tonight," I replied.

I stood up to leave. It wasn't quite 10:00 p.m., but I wanted to avoid any further dispute from other family members that might want to add to the conversation.

"I need to get going. I still need to go to my apartment and change so I can be at the food plant by 11:30. I have to start draining the entire system to replace a boiler. The crew will be there at 6:00 a.m., and draining the system takes at least four hours if everything goes smoothly. Things never go smoothly, and if they do, it's because God has something worse planned when we are out of time," I informed my family as I went to leave. I gave my hugs, said my farewells, and left.

My brother was in a unique position to have that discussion with me. He and his future wife took me to Shreveport, Louisiana, for my twenty-second birthday to do some gambling. I didn't want to go because I didn't want to take the three days off work. I also had never been to a casino and didn't like the idea of gambling my hard-earned money away. I didn't mind betting on a pool table because that was a game of skill, and I was good enough to win more than I lost. But the casinos to me were more a matter of chance, not skill, and I had always heard the odds were in the house's favor.

My brother wouldn't take no for an answer, though, and came to the construction site to basically kidnap me. My time as a plumber had taught me to always keep an extra change of clothes in my truck because you never knew when things may get icky. So, I grabbed my bag and tossed it in my brother's brand-new BMW 500 series wagon.

"Hold on, I need to go talk to Tom," I said to my brother when I tossed my bag in the car.

I walked over to Tom's truck. As I approached, he rolled down his window and said, "Everything okay, Mikey?"

"Yes, sir. That's my brother. He has come to take me to

Shreveport for the weekend. Guess I won't be working tomorrow," I said, my head hanging a bit.

"Shit, Gump, you look like someone just told you your dog died," Tom reached in his pocket and pulled out a twenty, "put this on eleven black on the roulette table and try to have some fun. I'll call Mike Callan for you and let him know you didn't see this coming."

My brother, his future wife, and I pulled out of the parking lot a little after 4:30 p.m., and I drove the whole way. I remember we listened to Candlebox pretty much the entire time. After we checked into our rooms in Shreveport, I took a shower and changed into my spare clothes. Luckily, it was a fresh pair of Levi's and a nice Wrangler pearl-snap that just needed a little ironing. After getting settled, my brother and his future wife took me to the casino floor. My brother took me toward the blackjack tables, and his future wife headed to the craps table.

We sat down at one of the five-dollar tables and, in less than half an hour, I had lost forty dollars. I looked at my brother and said, "Do you know how long I have to work to make forty bucks? Two hours; I have to work two hours to make forty dollars, and I just lost it in thirty minutes." I was genuinely distraught.

"What the hell are you complaining about? I gave you that money to lose," my brother said with a laugh.

"I know, but I could have taken the three hundred dollars you gave me and turned it into possibly 500 on the pool table at Woody's," I said in despair.

"And do what with it?" my brother asked.

"I don't know. Something a hell of a lot more fun than losing it in half a damn hour," I replied.

"You've played five hands, Michael," he said. "You need to loosen up. Here, let's get some shots in you." After a few shots and some schooling on playing blackjack in the hotel room, we gave the tables another chance. I started to win a little and drank a lot. I admittedly did end up having fun, but I never went back to the casinos after that trip.

I think it was December 27th, 2003, when my brother called and said that he, his future wife, and one my sisters had gone in together on a timeshare in Cozumel. "We are going there on January 9th for a week-long vacation, and you're coming with us. Tell your boss you'll need the ninth through the fourteenth off," my brother said.

"I don't know. A lot is going on at work right now. I don't think it's a good time for me to be taking a vacation," I argued.

"Michael, from the looks of it, it's never going to be a good time. You haven't had a real vacation since you started working there. I think you're due. Now call your boss, or I will," my brother said emphatically.

I wasn't sure my brother would really call Mike Callan, but then I wasn't quite sure he wouldn't either. Len was standing next to me when my brother called and, after I hung up, said, "I didn't hear all of it, but I heard enough. I don't care where they want to take you, Mikey; you're going on that vacation. I'll tell Mike Callan to fire your ass for a week if you try to say no."

After I thought about it for a little bit and let the idea settle in, a warm beach in Cozumel sure sounded better than the cold concrete of the construction site we were working on. I pulled up the calendar on my phone and checked the dates. I did some quick math in my head then called Mike Callan.

"Hey, Mikey. What can I do for you?" Mike answered.

"Well, sir, do you have a second?" I asked.

"I do now. You're not quitting, are you?" he joked.

"No, sir. My brother has informed me that I need a vacation. So, on January 9th, I am headed to Cozumel for a week. I have already looked at the calendar. If I can, I would like to use two days of vacation, and I'll bank my overtime from Christmas for the other three days?" I asked politely, then waited. I fully expected to be told a week was too long to be gone.

"I think that's a great idea, Mikey. You do need a vacation. Your requested use of time is approved, also. Just remind me between now and the ninth; I might forget," Mike said.

"Yes, sir, I will. And thank you," I replied and ended the call.

Every day for the next two weeks, I reminded Mike Callan of my upcoming trip. He must have started getting annoyed. Because after a week, if he saw me or called on the phone, he would start the conversation with, "I know you're going to Cozumel on the ninth."

The ninth finally arrived, and I went to my brother's house around 8:00 a.m. to ride to the airport together. I wasn't at my brother's for more than a few minutes when my phone rang. It was Old Man Tom.

"Where the hell are you, Gump?" Tom yelled through the phone as I answered.

"What are you talking about? I am about to leave on vacation," I responded.

"What? You better call Mike. He thinks you're supposed to be out here at the Chip Factory helping me," Tom said, then hung up.

"What the hell?" I murmured under my breath. But my brother must have heard.

"What's wrong?" my brother asked.

"I don't know. Mike Callan told Tom I was supposed to be helping him at one of the food plants today. I am calling Mike Callan now," I replied.

"Where the hell are you, Gump?" Mike yelled through the phone when he answered.

"At my brother's house about to..." I started, but Mike interrupted.

"It's after eight in the damn morning on a Thursday, and you're at your brother's house? Why the hell aren't you at work?" Mike said.

"Well, sir, it's..." I tried, but Mike interrupted again.

"It's the ninth, and you're leaving for vacation. Have fun, Mikey. I just wanted you to remind you why you're taking a vacation," he said with a laugh and hung up the phone.

"Holy shit! Is it too early to start drinking?" I said aloud, laughing and shaking at the same time.

"No. That's why there are drinks like screwdrivers and bloody marys. Everything okay?" my brother asked.

"Yeah, just the guys at work, letting me know I'll be missed. Or, giving me a reason to stay in Cozumel," I laughed as I poured vodka with a bit of orange juice into a glass.

By 10:00 a.m., everyone going to Cozumel had arrived at my brother's house and loaded their bags into his Suburban. My brother's neighbor came over to act as our chauffeur, and we headed to the airport. Our group consisted of my brother, his future wife, my sister, two others that were the future sister-in-law's friends, and me.

When we landed in San Miguel, Cozumel, we all grabbed our bags and a margarita. We then got on a shuttle service provided by our resort. I am not completely certain, but I think I was the only person in the group who spoke enough Spanish to bridge the communication gap between resort staff and ourselves. Being able to bridge that gap became quite beneficial in many ways.

The first night after dropping our bags in our rooms and placing our valuables in the rooms' safes, we went down to the large cabana bar in the center of the resort. I must have forgotten we would be there for a week because I tried to drink all the tequila in Cozumel on the first night. I threw up twice but continued to drink after each time. Finally, I admitted defeat and stumbled to my room. Apparently, Cozumel has a lot of tequila. The next morning, we all went to breakfast together, but after I set out to explore the resort. I wanted to test how far an all-inclusive would reach. I took a kayak across the quarter mile of shallows to the reef. The shallows at their deepest might have been twenty-feet-deep, but on the other side of the reef, it was a several-thousand-feet-drop. I spent the morning snorkeling in the shallows, then decided to get some lunch and begin my second round of drinking. I did much better pacing myself this time, though. I didn't start doing shots until after dinner.

I had dinner with the group but then decided I wanted to head into San Miguel and explore the city for a bit. I took a ferry across to

Playa Del Carmen, bar hopped for about an hour, and caught another ferry back. When I got back to San Miguel, I strolled into the Hard Rock Cafe. At first, there was barely a crowd, but it didn't take long for that to change. Soon after my third shot at the Hard Rock I heard a group with Texas accents and decided to introduce myself. After I purchased a few rounds of shots, they began counting me as a member of their party. About an hour and several shots later, my new group decided they wanted to go back to their resort and have a party on the beach. They extended an invitation, and I happily accepted. Their resort was adjacent to mine, and I had really hit it off with a member of their party named Courtney.

"I'll have to meet y'all on the beach. I need to go to my place and change," I said to the group.

"Then I'll share a cab with you and make sure you don't get lost," Courtney offered.

Courtney and I left the Hard Rock, got a cab, and headed to my resort. The taxi dropped us at the front, and I led Courtney to my room as we made small talk.

"Wow, nice place," Courtney said as we walked into the room.

"Thanks," I replied.

The room was quite lovely. It was on the third floor and fairly large. It had tile floors and two queen-sized beds. There was a large balcony that had a round table with four chairs, each large enough to hold two people. The balcony faced west over the palm trees, across the fifty-or-so-yards of the beach, and out into the bay.

"There's some Del Sol in the fridge if you want a beer. I am going to step into the bathroom and change real quick," I said to Courtney.

"Okay, thanks. I'll get you one, too," she replied.

I finished changing and joined Courtney on the balcony. The night sky was clear; a light breeze blew through the leaves of the palms giving a rhythm to the sound of waves keeping the beat. I walked up next to Courtney and leaned against the balcony's wooden railing. Courtney handed me the beer she had gotten for me, inched a little closer, and we watched as a cruise ship passed quietly through the bay headed into port at San Miguel.

"This really is a great place," Courtney said quietly.

"Yeah, it's mine until Tuesday," I smiled as I lifted the beer to my lips.

"We leave Sunday," Courtney returned.

"Well, at least we have until then," I replied and looked at Courtney. I held my beer up as a toast. Courtney pushed my beer aside, leaned into me, and we kissed passionately.

"We had better head down the beach before we get carried away," Courtney said, her lips only centimeters from mine.

"Yeah, we wouldn't want that," I replied with a smile, then kissed her a little more.

As we walked back into the room from the balcony, I turned on the balcony light, hoping it would act as a beacon when I headed home. We walked down the set of stairs that led to the beach, continued through the palm trees, and onward until the waves were just lapping over our ankles. Then we turned left and began our journey along the beach. In the distance, we could see a low glow from a fire. We finished our beers just as we reached the last beach-side cabana bar of my resort. We exchanged our empties for two new ones and continued our trek. The walk took a little more than an hour to complete because, naturally, we had to stop and test the temperature of the waters.

We arrived at the party, and the fire we had seen when we started our walk was indeed that of Courtney's group. The fire was more extensive now than before, and there was more alcohol on hand than any group of people ever should need. Courtney and I went for several swims between shots. The music could barely be heard from the edge of the water, and the glow from the fire danced on our skin. The setting was perfect, but, unfortunately, tequila would strike again. Not me this time, but Courtney.

Around 4:00 a.m., Miss Courtney had one too many shots and had to visit a palm tree for relief. I accompanied her to make sure she didn't pass out and hold her hair. When she was done, I walked her to her room. I had to physically carry her the last little bit. When we arrived at her door, I found her room key, then carried her to her bed. I placed the bathroom trash can next to the bed and left my phone number on the notepad siting on the nightstand. I hadn't had the foresight to ask her for hers before now. I left her room and went back to the beach to head home.

As I passed the party, someone handed me a shot. I accepted it and a couple of more as I said goodbyes. Then I began the short trek back to my end of the beach with a beer for the road. I had made it about halfway when the desperate need for a restroom hit my bladder. Unfortunately, there were none, so I thanked God for blessing me with manhood and utilized a tree. While I stood there creating a body of water of my own, God decided to say you're welcome by dropping a coconut onto my shoulder. I looked up, laughed, and said to the stars, "Luckily, I am drunk, or that would've hurt. Jokes on you, though, that barely grazed me."

God must not have thought that was funny because suddenly, I began to feel the last couple of shots I had taken. First came the flash of cool sweat that just beads out of your pores. Then the battle with my stomach trying to keep down all that was wanting to come up. I wasn't a rookie, though; I didn't try to fight it long. I stumbled over to another tree, dropped to my knee, and dug a small hole in the sand. I stood back up to avoid any splash, held on to the tree, and let my body discharge the sin I had filled it with. I completely missed the hole.

I tried to hold on to the tree, but the world began to spin. I realized that this would also be a battle I would lose and quickly put distance between me and those trees. I stumbled a few feet toward the sound of the waves, then fell to the ground. The sand was soft and cool. I managed to focus on a lounge chair long enough to crawl over to it, but then the world began to spin with more velocity. Now my fascination with astronomy, which was usually a blessing when talking to ladies, became a curse for me. A thought crept into my mind, "The earth spins at over 1,000 miles per hour. It will fling you off if you don't hold on." With that, I began to panic. I clenched the sand with one hand, grasped the lounge chair with the other, and held on as tightly as possible. I could feel the earth's rotation attempting to fling me into outer space. "God, please, I don't want to fall off the earth," I cried out. Then, almost as quickly as the spins came, they began to dissipate. I regained enough strength to flop myself into the lounge chair. "I'll just rest here a minute, then continue on," I whispered.

I awoke a few hours later to the hot Cozumel sun beating down on my dehydrated body. I opened my eyes to a now well-populated beach. Many of those passing by looked at me with disdain and disgust, while others merely laughed.

"What's the big deal? Surely, I can't be the first person they have seen passed out on this beach?" I thought to myself.

A cool breeze came off the ocean onto the perspiration that coated my body, and it felt nice. Then I noticed, to my horror, that I felt the breeze somewhere I shouldn't. I looked down and now understood all the looks and laughs. After using the first palm tree, the tequila's revenge came on so quickly that I never tucked the manhood I was so thankful for back into my shorts. My face was sunburned enough to mask my embarrassment, but unfortunately, so was the portion of me that hadn't seen the sun since my infancy. I calmly stood up, put my embarrassment away, and continued my stroll back to my room. I hadn't made it as far as I had thought, though. The lounge chair I rose from was still on Courtney's resort, and my room was on the opposite end of the beach.

Needless to say, I didn't venture to that end of the beach for the rest of the trip. That didn't keep me safe from embarrassment, though. A couple of days later, I took a three-hundred-dollar crash course in scuba diving. After our sixty-five-meter-deep dive along the reef, my very attractive, very athletic dive instructor agreed to join me for a drink. She began telling me a funny story she had heard from one of her friends on another resort. It was about a guy passing out on the beach with his verga hanging out. When my face began turning red, she instantly knew I was that guy, and I hung my head in shame.

"Hey, it's okay. You're muy famoso," my dive instructor said.

"Great, I am famous. You want to go out tonight with someone famous for that?" I asked.

She looked at the gentleman behind the little cabana bar we were sitting at and said, "Dos tequila mas por favor."

She handed me one of the shots and whispered with a smile, "Si, maybe you become famoso, mas."

PART TWO: NEW YORK CITY

I returned home from Cozumel on Tuesday, January 14th, eager to get back to work so I could get some rest. Like many who visit Mexican resorts, I vowed never to drink again. That vow, however, would not survive through the weekend.

I reported back to Geep Mechanical on Thursday, January 16th, because Thursdays were the beginning of a new pay period. I had spoken to Mike Callan the day before, and he instructed me to be at the office by 8:00 a.m. I got to the shop a little before 7:00 a.m. and helped Termite unlock the shop gates. Termite and I talked a bit about my vacation over a cup of coffee, then at 8:00 a.m., I walked into Mike Callan's office. I sat down in one of the two chairs next to his desk and waited for him to complete a series of what appeared to be morning rituals which ended with pouring a cup of coffee. Once he was settled in his office chair, he looked at me and said, "How are you this morning, Mikey?"

"Pretty exhausted after watching that production," I laughed.

"Yeah, that's nothing. I work harder getting out of bed and to my truck than you do all day," Mike retorted.

"Well, where should I go this morning?" I asked.

"You need to go visit Your Baby, Gump. She's missed you, and Tim has a list for you," Mike answered.

"Great. I guess no one has been working on it while I've been gone?" I asked.

"No. Not really. Tim would call about a leak, and I would send someone to put on a temporary fix," Mike answered.

"Well, that sounds awesome," I said sarcastically. "I guess I'll head there and see if it's floated away."

I left the office and drove the ten minutes to the plant, dreading the disaster that lay ahead. If constant attention to My Baby kept me busy almost every night, I couldn't imagine what a week of neglect would look like. I arrived at the plant around 8:40 a.m. and knew Tim wouldn't make it to the maintenance shop until 9:00, so I went over to the break area where a small group of maintenance workers was gathered. I had another cup of coffee and listened to them explain where some of the leaks were. Tim came strolling in right on time, and when he saw me, a smile stretched across his face like I was a long-lost family member. As we walked toward each other, Tim handed me a box of donuts he was holding then hugged me.

"Hey, Mikey. Thank God you're back," Tim said, still hugging me.

"Surely, it can't be that bad?" I questioned.

We walked to Tim's office, and as he unlocked his door, he responded, "You better have a couple of donuts, Mikey; you're going to need your strength."

Not one to turn down free food, I followed his suggestion. I placed the box of donuts on a table opposite his desk, and when I turned around, Tim was handing me a binder.

"What's this, a new safety log?" I asked.

"No, that's everything leaking that needs to be fixed. Every time one of the maintenance guys was called to a leak or found one, they added it to a list with a location. I spent all day yesterday typing the list out, organizing it by priority, just for you," Tim replied.

"Thanks, I guess?" I said tentatively.

I held in my hands a black, three-ringed binder that resembled a new OSHA code. The list was seventeen pages front and back.

"Do you want a guy to walk around with you to show you everything?" Tim asked.

"No. The descriptions seem good enough. I'll find what I can, and if I miss any, then I'll ask. Right now, I need to call Mike Callan and let him know I am going to be out here for the rest of my life," I answered jokingly.

I ate my donuts and talked to Tim about my trip, leaving out the exposure incident, then went to my truck to call Mike.

"Hey, Gump. How's your Baby?" Mike asked as he answered with a chuckle.

"Well, at least it's still standing," I started. "I'll probably be out here all day today and most of tomorrow scouting the seventeen pages of shit I have to fix. I will also need to leave the construction site we are working on a little early each day. I am sure most nights, something else will pop when I turn the system back on, creating a new priority."

"Okay, I'll call Tom and talk to him to make sure he understands. Oh, and Mikey. Welcome back," Mike Callan finished, then hung up.

For the next few months, I played catch-up, once again working an average of eighty-plus hours a week. The idea of taking a weekend off wasn't even a consideration, not even Sundays. Of course, this didn't go unnoticed. One day about a month into the Herculean task, Len and I went to lunch while I was spending the day at a construction site he was on.

"You look tired, Mikey," Len said.

"I am. I was out at My Baby again last night," I replied.

"No, not just that kind of tired. Worn out, tired. Like you already need another vacation, tired. I swear you've aged a year in the last month. And is that grey hair?" Len said.

"Yeah. That's what I get for taking a week off," I replied with a grin.

"That's bullshit, Mikey. You're not the only plumber Geep has. You're just the only that will work nights, weekends, and everything in between. If you would just say no once in a while, they would get someone else," Len argued.

"Exactly, then I might lose all the overtime," I snapped.

"That's bullshit too, and you know it," Len returned, then changed the subject before he really became upset.

Another month passed, and still I worked to complete Tim's list while also conquering other emergencies that arose. One night I was awakened by a phone call at 12:30 a.m. For once, it wasn't Mike Callan. Instead, it was my youngest sister, so I answered immediately. Though she was my youngest sister, she was still sixteen years my elder.

"What's up, sis?" I answered.

"Sorry to wake you. But for some reason, my garage door won't open. I think it's off the track. I gave mom my house key so she could clean while I was out of town. Can you come let me in?" my sister asked.

My sister travelled three or four days a week because she was a district manager of a high-end clothing company. My mother had recently retired, so all five children paid her to clean our homes. If we didn't pay her, she would still clean them.

"Yes, of course. I'll be right there," I assured my sister. It would take more time to get dressed than it would for me to drive to her house. I put on some work clothes, got in my truck, then remembered I only had a garage door opener. If hers wasn't working, then mine wouldn't either, so I called my sister back.

"Hey, sis, you know all I have is a garage door opener, right?" I said when I heard her answer.

"No. You don't have a key?" she asked in despair.

"No, ma'am," I replied.

"Okay. I'll go over to mom and dad's and get my key from them," my sister sighed.

"Nah, I am already awake, dressed, and in my truck. I'll go over and get it if you call dad and let him know I am on my way," I said with a yawn.

"Okay, thank you, Michael," my sister replied.

Half an hour later, I arrived at my sister's house with the key. I got out of my truck and walked to my sister's car to carry her suitcase. I could tell she had been crying.

"What's wrong?" I asked.

"It's just been an awful day. My flight was delayed, and I missed my connection. Then I get home and can't get in the house," my sister answered, trying to hold back more tears.

"Oh. I am sorry. Here I'll get you in, then fix your garage real quick," I said sympathetically.

"Okay, thank you," she replied.

I unlocked my sister's front door then carried her suitcase to her room. She went over to her bar and made herself a vodka on the rocks while I went out to the garage. The roll-up door had indeed come off the track, so with a lift and a shove, it was fixed. I opened and shut it a couple of times to ensure it stayed fixed, then got my sister's car keys and pulled her car into the garage. I went in the house to return her keys, and my sister was already on her second drink. I went to the kitchen to make myself half a pot of coffee, and my sister came over to the bar-top island to tell me what had led to her tears in more detail.

"I visited three stores today," my sister began, "and all of them were a disaster. None of the window displays were correct, and the floor displays looked like a teenage boy's room. One of the general managers didn't show up to work again, so now I have to terminate her. Which is my least favorite thing, not including the paperwork. Then I get to the airport, and there's a short delay boarding, then another when we landed in Chicago. Of course, my connecting flight is on the other end of the damn world, and when I get there, the plane is pushing away from the terminal." My sister got up to take another drink, but I offered to make it for her. Then she continued. "I had to wait three hours for the next flight, which was also delayed at both ends. Finally, I got in my car and drove home. All I wanted was a drink and my own bed, but instead, I couldn't get into my damn house. I call you thinking you have a key, only to find out you don't, UUGGHH!" my sister finished.

"Well, I hate to make things worse, but you're out of vodka, too," I said.

"What?" my sister yelled.

"Just kidding," I said, setting the drink in front of her as I began to laugh.

"That's not funny, asshole," she laughed.

"You're lucky I was home. I am supposed to be fixing leaks at a food plant right now, but I must have slept through my alarm," I said.

"Oh no. Are you going to be in trouble?" my sister asked.

"No, it's not a big deal. I will call Mike Callan in a few hours and tell him. It's Friday anyway. The things I was going to fix today I can just add to the list for tomorrow," I answered.

"Okay. Yeah, it is lucky you were home. I would have had a total meltdown otherwise," my sister added.

I looked at my watch, and it was just after 2:00 a.m.

"Well, I am going to take off. I can beat traffic and be at the construction site by 2:30, which will get me four more hours of sleep before the day begins," I said.

"Okay. I am going to finish this drink and head to bed. Want to meet at Fox and the Hound later? I'll buy you a couple of drinks to thank you for coming to the rescue," my sister offered.

"Hell yeah, that sounds great. I'll call you when I get home from work," I replied.

I left, drove to the construction site, and quickly fell asleep in my truck. The alarm on my cell phone went off at 6:30 a.m., and I called Mike Callan.

"Good morning, Mikey. How did things go out at the plant?" Mike asked.

"Pretty good, I guess. I overslept and didn't make it out there. Sorry," I replied.

"Oh, okay. Well, no one called, so I assume the place is still standing. How close are you to being done with Tim's list?" Mike asked.

"Only a few pages left. So long as nothing major breaks, I should be able to finish in a few weeks," I answered.

"Okay. I'll call Tim and let him know. What time are you working tomorrow?" Mike asked.

"About nine or nine-thirty. I want to sleep in a little," I replied.

"Okay, do you want to work Sunday at the Sausage Factory?" Mike questioned.

"I don't want to, but I will. Why, what's going on there?" I replied.

"Tom is working out there, and it wouldn't hurt to have you show up. I have Chad and Charlie on board, too, but you know how they are," Mike said.

"Yeah. I'll tell Tom I'll be there. He just pulled into the job," I told Mike.

"Okay, great. Have a good weekend, Mikey," Mike laughed, then ended the call.

I grabbed my empty coffee cup and walked over to Tom's truck. Tom rolled down his window as he saw me approach.

"What's up, Gump?" Tom asked.

"Hey, Tom, can I have a shot of coffee?" I asked, holding my cup out like Oliver Twist.

"Sure. Another long night at your Baby?" Tom questioned, pouring me half a cup from his green, metal Coleman thermos.

"No, I overslept. But my sister called about 12:30 and was in a bit of a pickle. So, I helped her out," I replied.

"Damn, that sucks. Oversleep just to be woken by a sibling in need. You can catch a break, kid," Tom said.

"True, but had she not called, I may have slept straight through the day," I replied.

"Yeah. That might not be a bad thing, Mikey. You look like shit. Are you working tomorrow?" Tom asked, letting a trail of tobacco spit out the window.

"Yeah, at My Baby. Then with you at the Sausage Factory, Sunday," I answered.

"What? Why? Chad and Charlie should be plenty," Tom questioned.

"Mike asked me to be back up in case they don't show. You know how they tend to be late or not show up at all," I replied.

"If they don't show, then I'll go home. Maybe then Mike will fire their asses," Tom responded.

"Yeah, well, if they do show up, then I'll go home," I laughed.

"Well, if you don't slow down, Mikey, you'll die of old age before me. Just letting you know, even I can tell," Tom finished as he stepped out of his truck.

"Good, then I might get some sleep," I laughed and went back to my truck to return my cup and get my tools.

Tom and I began our work, and at 5:00 p.m. the day was done. I drove to my apartment, showered, and called my sister.

"Hey, Michael," my sister answered.

"Hey. What are you doing?" I asked.

"Just sending an email to HR about terminating that general manager. What are you doing?" my sister replied.

"Making a drink at my apartment. Do you still want to meet at The Fox?" I asked.

"Yes! I just need to finish this, and I am done. I can meet you there at about seven o'clock," my sister answered.

"Okay. Do you want to play pool? If so, I can get there early to get a table," I offered.

"Yeah, that would be good. Are you working tomorrow?" she asked.

"Of course. But I am not going in until 9:00 a.m., so we can hang out a bit before I go to Woody's. You're welcome to come, too, of course," I replied.

"We'll see; I might meet up with some friends downtown. I'll see you in a bit," she finished.

I hung up my cordless phone and looked at my watch. It was

6:00 p.m., and the Fox and the Hound wasn't even five minutes away. So, I made another Cuba Libre and sat on the couch to watch an episode of "Friends."

The Fox and the Hound called itself an Irish pub, but it was actually a somewhat high-end billiards bar. It had nine large tournament-size pool tables, rented by the hour, and several dartboards in their own area. It also featured a large, granite-topped bar that rolled out in a half circle overlooking a decent-sized dining area. The Fox and the Hound served everything from typical bar food like chicken tenders and buffalo wings to higher-end food like steak and baked potatoes. The steak wasn't the best in town, but it wasn't the worst. Like many places on the west side of Fort Worth with a pool table, I visited the Fox often — usually, in late afternoon on a weekday when on my way home from work. I would stop in to practice a little pool by myself, have a drink or two, and decompress from a challenging day. Because of my ritual, I became known and liked by most waitresses and bartenders. I almost always got a pool table for free, and half of my drinks would mysteriously disappear from my tab. This happened because the wait staff knew that the lower my tab was, the more I would tip. Quite often I would tip more than the tab.

I arrived at the Fox and the Hound about 6:45 p.m. and went up to the bar.

"I was wondering if we were going to see you tonight," the bartender said.

"Yeah, I am meeting my sister here for a couple of drinks and some pool," I replied.

"Cool, I'll keep an eye out and send her over. Ashley is holding a set of pool balls for you. Do you want your usual?" the bartender inquired.

"Yes, please. Thank you. You're my favorite bartender. But don't tell the other bartenders I said that," I replied with a wink and a smile.

I got my drink and went to where they issued pool balls. I visited with Ashley for a bit before claiming my set and going to the only table left. I saw my sister walk in a little after 7:00 p.m. Once she paid a visit to the bartender, she came over to my table. In her hands were a fresh Bacardi and coke with lime for me and vodka with water and lime for herself. I began collecting the pool balls scattered on the pool table and racking them together. Like most McGarreys, my sister was pretty proficient in the game of pool.

"Hey, Michael. How long have you been here?" my sister asked.

"About fifteen minutes," I replied.

"Oh, how many drinks have you had?" she questioned further.

"This one," holding the glass in my hand up, "is my second, and the one you put on the table will be my third," I answered.

"Okay, awesome. I had better play you quick then," my sister replied.

My sister was the only person in the world that knew I had a window when it came to my pool prowess. That window stayed firmly shut until after I had three adult beverages and at least two warm-up games. Because my sister was aware of this, she knew she still had a chance to beat me before my window opened.

"What time did you wake up this morning?" I asked.

"About ten o'clock. I can't thank you enough for getting the key and everything else," my sister replied.

"No problem. Do you want to break?" I offered.

"Sure," she answered as she chose a pool stick from the wall-mounted rack.

My sister broke but didn't make anything. I grabbed my pool cue, took a drink, and as I passed her to take my turn, she said, "You look like crap, Michael. When was the last time you slept?"

"I slept this morning in my truck, thanks to you," I replied as I lined up my shot.

"Okay, let me rephrase the question. When was the last time you had a day off?" my sister pressed further.

I walked to the drink table after my turn and answered, "I don't know. A couple of months ago, I guess."

"Don't tell me not since Cozumel?" my sister asked, moderately shocked.

"Well, maybe," I replied as I lit a cigarette knowing the conversation was going to get more sensitive from here.

"Jesus, Michael! Why?" she continued.

"Well, the entire time we were in Cozumel, a food plant I am somewhat responsible for was neglected. So, I have had a lot of catching up to do. Unfortunately, I can only catch up between midnight and 4:00 a.m. on weekdays and during the days on weekends. But while I am catching up, other stuff breaks. It's a never-ending struggle," I replied, taking a long pull off my smoke.

"That sucks. You need another vacation," my sister said.

"No. I need another me," I grinned. "But I am almost caught up. I should be able to slow down in a couple of weeks." I finished my drink and began the one my sister had bought.

"I am going to Manhattan on April 25th for a week. You should come, too. My company is paying for everything, we'll just share the hotel room. You just need to buy the plane ticket. In fact, I think I can get the ticket with my miles," my sister offered.

"That actually sounds like a lot of fun. I'll tell Mike Callan on Monday. He'll probably have a damn stroke," I replied.

The weekend progressed as expected. Neither Chad nor Charlie showed up at the Sausage Factory on Sunday. Still, Tom and I were able to complete the assigned tasks reasonably quickly. On Monday, late morning, I called Mike Callan at the office.

"This can't be good," Mike said as he answered, "you never call me on the office phone."

"I am going on vacation April 25th, for a week, to Manhattan," I said.

"Kansas or New York?" Mike asked.

"New York. That's a month-and-a-half from now, so I'll bank whatever overtime I need to cover what my remaining vacation time won't," I replied.

"Okay, Mikey, it's in the books. Is that all?" Mike responded.

"Yes, sir. From my end, anyway," I answered.

"Okay, have a nice day. And, Mikey, tell Charlie and Chad to call me if you see them," Mike Callan finished and hung up.

A few weeks went by, and I had finally caught up at work. My upcoming vacation was still a month away, but now I had most Sundays off. One night, during this slow period, my sister invited me to a bar in Arlington called Sherlock's with my other sister and one of their friends. She invited me because Sherlocks was another higher-end billiards bar much like the Fox and the Hound, except Sherlocks had quarter-fed, bar-room pool tables, which were great for hustling. Also, I had never been there, so no one would know me. I rode with my siblings and their friend, Christina. When we arrived, we all went to the bar for drinks, but after I received mine, plus some quarters, I quickly headed to the pool tables.

When my sisters and I went out together, we quickly separated. Partly because they were sixteen and seventeen years older than me. Also, even though they were that much older, the three of us looked close in age, and we didn't want to cramp the others' styles.

After being at Sherlock's for about an hour, I was sitting on an air hockey table flirting with a waitress while waiting on my turn to play a pool game. I looked over and saw my two sisters and Christina walking towards me, single file, wearing on their faces giant shit-eating grins. I took a long pull from my Cuba Libre and asked the waitress to get me another. I didn't know what was coming, but I was certain I didn't want her to bear witness. Unfortunately, the waitress didn't leave quickly enough.

"You know, Michael, you would be a really good-looking guy if you would just learn how to dress," Sixteen blurted out.

I about spat my drink out, and the waitress said, "I'll get you a double," and she walked away.

"Excuse me?" I coughed. "What's wrong with how I dress?"

"For starters, pleated khakis and boots went out in the 90s. Also, you need shirts that fit better, and red isn't a good color on you," Sixteen replied.

"Also, Michael, you need a new hairstyle. Parted hair is for first-graders and old men," Seventeen added.

I looked at Christina, waiting for her to chime in.

"Oh, I just came to watch," Christina said with a laugh.

"I think you look okay," the waitress said, bringing my drink. "That one's on me," she placed a kiss on my cheek before walking away again.

"Michael, I work for a clothing company that gives me a fifty-percent discount. Let me take you shopping before we go to New York. If you don't notice a significant difference, you can return to your own style, and I'll never say anything else," Sixteen pleaded.

"And I'll take you to get a new hairstyle, but you have to trust me," Seventeen added.

"Okay. I am off tomorrow if y'all are free?" I asked.

"Works for us. We were hoping that's what you'd say," my sisters agreed.

"Are you pissed?" Christina asked.

"No. But I wish y'all would have told me before we came out. Or at least waited until I wasn't talking to the waitress," I answered.

"Oh no, this was a lot more fun to watch," Christina laughed.

The next day my sisters took me out for a rebuild. I had to step out of my comfort zone, and though I had my doubts, I did exactly as instructed. The following Friday night, I went to Sherlock's with my buddy Sam, dressed the way my sister had recommended. Not only did the waitress agree I looked ten times better, but two other ladies came over and talked for a while before giving me their phone numbers. Needless to say, for the next few years, I listened to my sisters when it came to style.

My sister and I arrived in New York around noon on Sunday, April 25th. We took a car from JFK to the Hudson Hotel located at 58th Street and 9th Avenue. We checked in and went to our room, where we found our first surprise.

The room was the size of a shoebox, with a king-size bed shoved in the center. The hallway ran from the door straight back to the bedroom, where it dead-ended at the bed's center. There were about six inches between the walls of the room and the edges of the bed. The bathroom was so small that I had to sit sideways and place my feet in the shower for me to sit on the toilet. Also, the designers of the shoe box decided the wall between the shower and the bedroom should be glass. My sister and I concluded the designers did this to make the shoebox appear larger. I am sure this was acceptable for a couple or someone staying alone. But my sister and I had to remember to close both curtains so that we didn't scar each other for life. The room was so small that the hotel didn't bother to furnish a remote for the seventeen-inch television mounted in the top right corner of the bedroom. A person as short as my five-foot-three sister could easily reach from the corner of the bed and change the channel.

"I hope you're not claustrophobic," my sister chuckled.

"I don't think I am, but then I haven't ever slept in a coffin, either," I laughed.

"I am going to call down and get a couple of more pillows sent up, so we can divide the bed," my sister stated as she picked up the phone mounted on the wall next to the door.

"Good idea. I don't think I move a lot when I sleep. But I never wake up in the same position I was in when I went to sleep," I said in agreement.

"Okay. I have to go to the corporate office to get ready for the meetings next week," my sister began, hanging up the hotel phone. "I'll take you to the subway in Columbus Circle and show you how that process works."

"Awesome. Sounds exciting," I responded nervously.

My sister and I left the shoe box, went down to 9th Avenue then walked to the subway at Columbus Circle and 9th Avenue. As we walked down the stairs to the subway, I felt I was in a scene from "Crocodile Dundee." There were so many people I could have tripped and not fallen to the ground.

"You have to be aggressive here, Michael; otherwise, you never make it anywhere. Think of it as a river. Find a current going the direction you want and hop in," my sister instructed loudly.

I did as I was told and hopped in behind my sister. We made our way down into the subway then to an automated kiosk. My sister inserted a twenty-dollar bill, and a few seconds later, a yellow card popped out with "Metro" written in blue.

"Here, take this and treat it like it's your golden ticket because it's your access to the subway," my sister said. She looked me in the eyes to ensure I understood its importance. "Now watch me refill mine."

I watched my sister complete a series of steps to refill her MetroCard, then she said loudly, "Got it?"

"I think so?" I replied, practically yelling to speak over the noises of the subway.

We walked over to a set of turnstiles with card readers mounted on top.

"Swipe your card in there," my sister shouted, pointing to the card reader.

So, I did.

"Don't just stand there; walk through," she yelled.

I pushed through the turnstiles then my sister pulled me to the side, "Michael, you have to get out of the Texan, slow-going mindset. You'll get trampled, and I don't want to explain to mom why I came home alone. This is a Sunday," she said, "the subway isn't even that busy. We'll ride the subway down to the next stop then I'll show you how to hail a cab."

My sister and I rode down to 50th and Broadway then walked up the stairs out of the subway. I watched my sister step halfway into the street, raise her hand like she needed to ask a teacher a question, then a few seconds later, a cab stopped in front of her.

"Get in," she said to me.

"Rockefeller Park," my sister told the cab driver, and we sped away.

The cab stopped at Rockefeller Park a few minutes later.

Rockefeller Park isn't to be confused with Rockefeller Center, by the way. I would learn that lesson later.

My sister handed the driver a twenty and instructed him to take me wherever I wanted, then looked at me and asked, "You got it? Are you going to be okay?"

"Yeah, I think so?" I answered with a little bit of doubt.

"You'll be okay. Getting around in Manhattan is best taught like teaching someone to swim. Throw them in the deep end and let them figure it out. Good luck," my sister finished. She stepped out of the cab, closed the door, and hurried away. It was now just the driver and me.

"Where to?" The driver asked.

"The Statue of Liberty seems like a good place to start," I answered.

"I can't drive you to Liberty Island, obviously, but I'll take you to the ferries in Battery Park. They will take you there," the cabby replied. Then like a shotgun, we were off.

The short drive to Battery Park was exhilarating, in the "I am going to die" sort of way. Clearly, the rules of driving I learned in Texas were merely recommendations in New York City. And the lane markers are suggestions rather than clear dividers.

When the cab dropped me at the ferries, the driver gave me directions on how to get to the boats then sped away. I lit a cigarette, took a minute to catch my breath, and took in the view of the harbor. I then proceeded to the ticket booth for the Liberty Island Ferries. The visit to the Statue of Liberty was inspiring and walking around Ellis Island was insightful.

After visiting the national monuments, I returned to Battery Park and walked north through the park. I came out at State Street and Broadway. Knowing Broadway was an iconic street, I decided to walk up it for a bit. I went to cross State Street and learned my next important lesson about Manhattan: if the crosswalk sign says, "Don't Walk," DO NOT WALK!

I thought I would be cool and dash across State Street before the sign said it was okay to cross. I had only taken two steps off the curb when suddenly I became a hood ornament on a taxi. Luckily, it wasn't going too fast, but it had enough speed that I landed on the hood when I leapt in the air like a damn deer. The cab driver hit the brakes, and I rolled off. My time as a bull rider in high school paid off because I landed on my feet, saving me from further embarrassment. I saw the Middle Eastern man exiting the driver's seat of the cab and raised my hand to signal I was okay. To my surprise, not only did the gentleman not care that I was okay, but he began issuing a string of profanities thoroughly questioning my intelligence. Once the exchange was complete, I continued to limp up Broadway a couple of blocks, hoping to put some distance between myself and any witnesses to the incident. Then decided to give hailing a cab a try.

I did as I had seen my sister do, and soon enough, a cab stopped in front of me. I got in and said, "The Empire State Building, please."

"Where are you from?" the cabby asked as we sped away.

"Texas. Why, is my accent that obvious?" I replied.

"No. You said please. People don't do that here," he responded.

The rest of the trip was silent until the cab came to an abrupt stop. Then the driver said, "That's two-fifty. The entrance is around the corner."

I paid and got out. I didn't have time to close the door before someone else got in, and the taxi was gone. I walked around the corner and along the sidewalk until I got to the next corner. "I didn't see an entrance. Maybe it's around the next corner," I thought to myself and continued walking. I continued around the block until I was back where I began, still no entrance to the Empire State Building. "Damn cab driver screwing with the tourist," I mumbled.

I crossed the street, hoping to see the iconic building but to no avail. All the sidewalks had construction scaffolding around them, covering the walkways and hindering my view. I walked several blocks and finally saw the Empire State Building. It was behind me in the direction I had just come from. I made a mental note of the direction and began walking. I got where the structure should be but once again, no joy. I walked around the block of 34th Street and 5th Avenue several times where the building was supposed to be, but for the life of me, I couldn't find the damn entrance. I hailed another cab, got in, and said, "The Empire State Building, please."

"What?" The driver asked.

"The Empire State Building," I repeated.

"It's right there," the driver said, pointing out the window.

"What? I've walked around that block five times and didn't see it," I replied.

"Didn't see it? What do you mean you didn't see it?" the driver asked.

"I got out in the street a little and looked up. I didn't see it," I said.

"You can't see it if you're right under it. That building is over eighty stories tall. You're a tourist, aren't you?" the driver laughed.

"Yes, sir," I answered.

"Here, I'll drive you around to the entrance for free," he offered.

The driver made two right turns, then stopped, "There's the entrance. See that little sign over the door?" The driver asked as he pointed out the window.

"Jesus, Mary, and Joseph. Yes. Thank you," I said and got out of the taxi.

Above a relatively standard, recessed doorway was a fairly insignificant sign hanging over the walkway; it said, "Empire State Building" with an arrow pointing to a door. I went inside and rode the elevators to the observation deck. The view was well worth the humiliation.

I left the Empire State Building and headed north, thinking I would walk back to the hotel. "It's only twenty-five blocks," I thought to myself. I began walking, looking at all the giant buildings. Suddenly, I found myself back at Battery Park. "Damn it," I mumbled. I had been walking south the entire time. The buildings were so large they blocked my peripheral view of the sun, rendering my internal compass useless. Of course, I hadn't been paying attention to the street signs because I was certain I was traveling in the right direction.

I turned around, correcting my mistake, and over the next few hours became more lost than a young goose. Through pure luck, I stumbled across the New York Stock Exchange, then to Ground Zero of the World Trade Centers. In 2004 Ground Zero was still an enormous hole in the ground, making the magnitude of 9/11 more real. From there, I somehow found Grand Central Station and then Times Square. While walking through Times Square, I was stopped by a guy pushing tickets to a venue.

"Hey, man, you look cool. How would you like a pair of free tickets to a comedy club?" He asked.

I laughed and said, "What's the catch? Nothing is ever free."

"No catch, just a two-drink minimum," the ticket guys replied.

"Okay. Where is it?" I asked, knowing my sister and I would easily bust the minimum.

"Comic Strip Live on 2nd between 81st and 82nd," he answered.

I took the tickets and said thank you, then continued walking. "I guess dressing like a J. Crew catalog puked on me worked out," I thought. I stumbled around Times Square and found a Hard Rock Cafe. Remembering my luck at the one in Cozumel, I walked in and sat at the bar, and started a conversation with the lovely bartender, whose name was, ironically, Courtney. After a few drinks and an entertaining conversation with Courtney, she offered to show me around the city. She only agreed to be my personal guide because she wanted to witness any further debacles firsthand after hearing about my first day.

Courtney was getting a shot of tequila in a souvenir shot glass for me when my sister called on my cell.

"Hey, how's it going?" my sister asked.

"Good, I am sitting at the Hard Rock near Times Square talking to the bartender," I replied.

"Of course, you are," my sister laughed. "I am leaving the office and getting a cab back to the hotel. Meet me in the hotel bar."

"Okay, will do," I replied and hung up.

"Was that your sister?" Courtney asked, returning with two shots, one for me and one for her.

"Yes, ma'am, it was," I replied.

"Boy, I sure could get used to your manners. Too bad you're only here for a couple of days," Courtney said.

"Yeah. Too bad indeed," I replied with a blushing smile. I raised my shot of tequila for a toast and waited until she raised hers and said, "Here's to short-lived moments becoming lifelong memories." We drank our shots then I asked, "Could you tell me how to get back to the Hudson Hotel from here?"

"Sure. You're on 43rd and 7th Avenue. You want to walk west on 43rd Street until you get to 9th Avenue then turn north and walk to 58th," Courtney said.

"Okay?" I replied hesitantly.

My confidence must not have been very convincing because Courtney added, "Here, I'll walk you out and point the way."

I eventually made it to the Hudson Hotel Bar and was in awe of what I saw. The floor was lit with white fluorescent tiles. There were a couple of couches, tables for standing, and a decent-size bar with top-shelf liquors. I saw my sister at the bar, so I walked to her with a nervous first step onto the glass floor.

"So, how was your first day?" my sister asked, handing me a Corona.

I told her all that had happened over a few drinks, and when she was through laughing, she asked, "Well, what do you want to do now?"

"Honestly, I would like to find a pool table and relax," I replied.

We asked the bartender where we might find a pool table, and he informed us the hotel had one in the Library. He gave us directions, and after ordering some drinks for the trip, we paid for our tab. It was then we learned how high-end the Hudson Bar was, "Eight dollars for a bottle of Corona and ten dollars for a shot of Patron," my sister said while looking at the tab.

"Looks like I'll be drinking Patron," I laughed.

The Library was really just a large lounge area decorated with several bookshelves adorned with hundreds of old-looking books. In the Library's center was the most oversized dark wood pool table I have ever seen. It had purple felt and braided dark brown leather pockets. Above the table was a sizable dome-shaped porcelain chandelier. It was pure porcelain white on the inside but a pool-table-felt green on the outside. When my sister and I walked in, there were already two gentlemen playing. My sister walked over to a nearby table as I approached one of the gentlemen and asked, "May I play the winner?"

"Absolutely," replied the gentleman in a noticeably feminine voice.

"Great, thanks," I said and walked over to my sister, then sat down.

"That's a big table," my sister whispered.

"It's not a real library," I whispered back. "But yeah, It's the largest I have ever seen," I finished in my usual tone.

Soon the gentlemen had finished their game and signaled it was my turn. I walked over, shook their hands, and introduced myself. I instantly had to apologize, though, because I had nearly broken their hands. I racked the pool balls as I had a million times before and waited for my opponent to break.

The gentleman broke and, after a few turns shooting, easily beat me. I played him and his partner several more times, but I played so poorly it appeared as though I had never held a pool cue. Finally, I accepted it wasn't my night, thanked the gentlemen for letting me play, then went back to my sister.

"What the hell just happened?" my sister asked, laughing.

"I was just humiliated doing the one thing I thought I could be sure of. I want to go home," I replied sarcastically, in a sad tone, wiping a fake tear from my eye.

"I wouldn't be too excited about getting home. I am telling everyone about this," my sister said, laughing even harder.

"Great," I replied, rolling my eyes. "I'll just deny it, and no one will believe you."

"Come on, we need to get a cab up to that comedy club. We can find a bar around there to ease the pain of your bruised ego," she ended with a laughing snort.

My sister and I did find an authentic Irish pub on the corner of 82nd Street and 2nd Avenue called O'Brady's. It had a regular bar-room-sized pool table where I redeemed myself. They also sold a more reasonably priced pint of beer for five dollars. The rest of the week went pretty smoothly, thanks to a couple of informative days with Courtney and some fantastic bars visited with my sister.

When my sister and I returned to Fort Worth and met up with my other siblings, my sister's first story was how a pair of extremely feminine men humiliated me on a purple pool table. It's a story she still brings up anytime I start getting a little too cocky on a pool table when playing against her.

CHAPTER 10

THE BIG CHANGE

GARY THE PUERTO RICAN

In the summer of 2006, I said goodbye to Geep Mechanical and by November was living in New York City with the same sister I had visited the Big City with in 2004. Ironically, we ended up in an apartment on 81st Street and 1st Avenue just one block from O'Brady's Irish pub, and it became the local establishment my sister and I visited almost every night to unwind from the hectic day of getting around and dealing with the New Yorker personalities.

My sister had moved to Manhattan to take a better position with her clothing company, and I moved there with her after she extended an invitation. I found work as a plumber a week after I arrived, and on the first day my supervisor said, "With your boiler experience, I am throwing you to the wolves." So, he gave me a helper, who would also be my driver while I learned the city, and assigned me a boiler room refabrication in a building owned by Columbia University.

My helper was a Puerto Rican I will call "Gary." It only took about half a day to determine that Gary was either a crackhead or a schizophrenic; my bet is on crack. But, not one to judge a person's life choices, I decided to do my best with him and teach Gary what I could.

It was about a week into the boiler job, and I had shown Gary how to solder copper. I had him solder some ¾-inch copper drain lines to let him practice while I prepared some four-inch copper to prefabricate when he was done. Suddenly I heard Gary yell, "It's going to blow!"

He ran up the stairs, got in the only elevator that went to the boiler room, and left. I walked around to where Gary was working and saw the hose of the acetylene tank on fire. Needless to say, working with Gary produced a couple of good stories.

I experienced dating in the big city and received another lesson in pool — this time by an old drunk Irishman. I lived in Manhattan for a little less than a year, but that time was amazing. The greatest lesson I learned by moving to New York City was that I didn't have to stay in Fort Worth, Texas. Not only was it okay to move out of state, but I learned that my soul needed to so I could continue to grow.

After moving back to Fort Worth in late spring 2007, I realized that my time in New York gave me the courage I needed to make my next big move. On January 9, 2008, I left for Fort Benning, Georgia, to begin a new life as a United States Army infantryman. While in the Army, I served with two prestigious units. First at 10th Mountain Division with Alpha Company, 4th Battalion, 31st Infantry Regiment — the Polar Bears — and then at 101st Air Assault Division with 1-75 Cavalry Squadron, also known as Bone Troop.

During my time with both units, I completed several training missions, a few military schools, a rotation at West Point training cadets, and a few deployments. Several drunken nights were so memorable that I still remember them, even though I had consumed enough alcohol that I shouldn't. There were also several events that — stone sober — were terrifying while they were happening but hilarious once everyone was proven to be okay.

I separated from the Army in the summer of 2014 and returned to Fort Worth, where I did a year and some change with the National Guard to finish my eight years of service. I picked up a job as a surveyor before getting hired as security at a large defense contractor. I landed the security job thanks to a friend of mine from high school named Chris Haw. While my infantry personality made me well qualified for the job, it also made me disliked by many of the senior staff, most importantly by the chief of security. But I made history with the lower security personnel when I humiliated the chief twice.

After a year and a half, I left the defense contractor and returned to plumbing life for about a year. I learned that a lot had changed in the plumbing world while I was gone. Everyone had become thin skinned and picking on people was no longer allowed. I found this out the hard way when I played a prank on one of my helpers, and he went crying to the boss. While my boss found it funny, he informed me that sort of thing was not permitted. Plumbing became dull, and I left the field for good.

I eventually moved to Tennessee to help an Army buddy get a cattle operation going. The timing couldn't have been better because I arrived at the ranch on February 4, 2020 — a month before COVID-19 hit. My buddy and I had a few hilarious moments, though. For example, a run-in with a one-eyed feral cow and a showdown with a very large rat inside a four-car garage that suddenly became too small for the three of us.

That will bring us to where I am now, writing my first pair of books. I have more living to do and many more memorable moments to experience. Still, I felt that the world could use something fun and light to read with everything going on.

So, if you found volume one fun and, in some cases, relatable, then hold on because things only get better from here. From sliding into my senior drill sergeant wearing nothing but my tighty-whiteys, to two combat veterans trying to herd a large rat out of a garage with shovels and brooms, there is plenty to look forward to.

About the Author

 Michael McGarrey is a Texas native that hails from the little big town of Fort Worth. He graduated from R.L. Paschal High School in 1999. While in high school, he worked as a baker at a cafeteria all four years and rode bulls independently for three years in high school and one year after he graduated.

After high school, Michael worked as a plumber in Fort Worth for a company that specialized in large industrial and commercial type plumbing. His primary focus was large food processing plants. Michael worked in Fort Worth as a plumber until 2006, when he moved to Manhattan, New York. Michael lived in New York for a year, where he also worked as a plumber. He was assigned a boiler room for Columbia University. Once completed, he had enough of New York and returned to Texas. Not able to find the kind of work he desired as a plumber; Michael decided to enter the United States Army as an Infantryman.

Michael graduated from One Station Unit Station from Fort Benning, Georgia, in May of 2008. Out of 54 men in the 3rd Platoon of 2/54, he was the only one chosen to go to the tundras of Fort Drum. He deployed to Iraq with the 10th Mountain Division, then

PCSed to 101st Airborne Division. He then deployed to Afghanistan with the 101 before exiting the military in late 2014.

After the army, Michael worked as a defense contractor in the U.S. before determining that his infantry personality wasn't conducive for corporate America. However, while working for said company, Michael got into recreational bodybuilding thanks to a good friend he knew from high school.

After leaving the defense contractor, he went back to work as a plumber. Only to find out that the construction world was now full of weak, thin-skinned people. And that while he still felt young most of the time, his back reminded him that 1 year in the Army Infantry adds 3 years to your body. So, he hung up his work boots, put on his cowboy boots, and moved to Tennessee to help an old army buddy start a cattle operation. After about half a year, that was done, and he decided to become a writer. He began by becoming a ghostwriter for companies that do question and answer articles on search engines. If you read an article about the best off-road tires for a Toyota Tacoma, or Tundra chances are he wrote it. His first book, titled "Life's Memorable Moments," will be two volumes of ten short stories each. The stories are about particular events in Michael's life, pre- and post-military, that Michael finds quite hilarious. Michael believes the world could use a little laugh, even if it's at him. And that people need to learn not to take themselves so seriously.

About the Publisher

Tactical 16 Publishing is an unconventional publisher that understands the therapeutic value inherent in writing. We help veterans, first responders, and their families and friends to tell their stories using their words.

We are on a mission to capture the history of America's heroes: stories about sacrifices during chaos, humor amid tragedy, and victories learned from experiences not readily recreated — real stories from real people.

Tactical 16 has published books in leadership, business, fiction, and children's genres. We produce all types of works, from self-help to memoirs that preserve unique stories not yet told.

You don't have to be a polished author to join our ranks. If you can write with passion and be unapologetic, we want to talk. Go to Tactical16.com to contact us and to learn more.

Made in the USA
Monee, IL
07 July 2026

56546304R00098